DEMOCRATIC PARTY ELITISTS

TOTALITARIAN WOLVES IN SHEEP'S CLOTHING

DEMOCRATIC PARTY ELITISTS

TOTALITARIAN WOLVES IN SHEEP'S CLOTHING

DAVID E. SCREWS

CITIOFBOOKS, INC.
3736 Eubank NE Suite A1
Albuquerque, NM 87111-3579
www.citiofbooks.com
Hotline: 1 (877) 389-2759
Fax: 1 (505) 930-7244

Ordering Information:
Quantity sales. Special discounts are available on quantity purchases by corporations, associations, and others. For details, contact the publisher at the address above.

Printed in the United States of America.

ISBN-13: Hardcover 978-1-960952-22-6

Library of Congress Control Number: 2023909747

Introduction

The elite of the American Democratic Party, the Clintons, Bernie Sanders, Barack Obama, Al Gore, and others, love to tell Americans that the greatest threat to humanity on the planet is "climate change." This assertion will be discussed in greater detail later in this work, but suffice it to say for the present that it simply is not the truth.[1] Global terrorism, primarily fomented by the Islamic State and other Islamic jihadists, and an insane dictator in North Korea rank among the greatest threats to human life.

What is likely the greatest threat to the security and happiness of Americans, and possibly the world, are the ideologues in the Democratic Party that utilize tactics employed by Vladimir Lenin and Josef Stalin to convince the voters that allowing the state increased levels of power is in their best interests. Both those men created a divisive climate within Russia by heightening tensions between the classes and creating enemies among themselves.[2] Matt Margolis and Mark Noonan explicitly described how Barack Obama deliberately and successfully divided Americans while alienating our allies abroad.[3]

Democrats are careful to avoid the use of the terms statism or communism because they are keenly aware of their negative connotations. However, socialism, the term they prefer to use even sparingly, is closely akin to both statism and communism. Statism refers to a condition in which a powerful central government controls all aspects of the economy, and the populace of said state must adhere to its dictates.[4] Mark Levin, in *Ameritopia: The Unmaking of America*, offers an excellent description of statism. "There are no inalienable rights," he says, except those deemed acceptable by the state. Labor and property belong to the state, "thereby enslaving the individual to the state."[5] This kind of thinking dovetails nicely with communism, as well as with much of the ideology of the Democratic Party. Fully believing their ideology will create the elusive utopian state, Democrats continue to clamor for greater state control of every aspect of our lives.

Perhaps Democrats, like Karl Marx, are simply ideologues who cannot fathom the true destructive nature of their agenda. Communism in the 20th century left in its wake the deaths of close to 100 million people because it was an inherently flawed ideology.[6] Since the United States remains the most powerful economic force on the planet, it stands to reason that if its economic institutions are dismantled, global destruction of human life will occur on a scale never before witnessed in the history of the world; it will be a holocaust far worse than what Hitler's Nazis committed in World War II. And much of the agenda of the Democratic Party either closely resembles communist/Marxist doctrine or it is explicitly Marxist in principle, and it is difficult for me to believe that the Democrats are not keenly aware of the disastrous results of what implementing Marxism in the Soviet Union, China, North Korea, and many other nations wrought on the populations of those states.

This work will utilize a historical frame of reference along with the scholarly works of contemporary authors to prove that Democrats are bent on imposing increased state authority over Americans by pressing an agenda not much different from that blueprinted by Karl Marx and Friedrich Engels in 1848. Marx and Engels, in a raging tirade against capitalism and industrialization, penned *The Communist Manifesto*, without regard for its consequences.[7] Why do Democrats seemingly discount the destructive nature of what Marx and Engels wrought?

Democratic Party proponents of government control of the economy have been around for more than a century. In the past they have argued that the flawed ideology of the state-run economy failed because Stalin and Mao didn't implement the system the way that Marx and Engels described it. While the revolutionary phases of the implementation of communism in China and Russia did not follow Marxist principles precisely, the leaders of both revolutions did, in fact, implement to varying degrees each and every one of the ten planks of communism, with calamitous effect for the people of those nations. More people died in Soviet gulags than were murdered in Hitler's concentration camps. Chairman Mao brutally crushed all opposition in China, while other Southeast Asian communist states, such as Pol Pot's Cambodia, ruthlessly murdered millions of their own citizens. Marx and Engels indeed, described the need to be brutal and ruthless in order to achieve their utopian worker's paradise.[8]

Utopias are unattainable. America's countercultural movement in the 1960s tried in vain to prove that Marx and Engels were correct. It was not the first time communal lifestyles had been attempted. Numerous societies, such as the Oneidas and New Harmony, were spawned by the Second Great Awakening in the United States in the 1830s and 1840s. All of them, without exception, failed due to sloth, jealousy, greed, and a number of other human frailties.

On a grander scale, the Soviet Union, the People's Republic of China, Cambodia, Cuba, North Korea, and other states, have proved that communism is an unworkable ideology. Given that fact from the historical record, why do Democrats continue to implement political and economic conditions that are very similar, if not precisely, the ideas put forth by Marx and Engels? There can be only one answer: they want total state control and, like Marx must have thought, believe there are no negative consequences. There are actually dire consequences for following Marxism, not the least of which is the loss of basic freedoms. Those who survive will be relegated to serfdom, peasantry in its basest form, or slavery; yes, even slavery. Remember the gulags in the USSR? The powerful will be the only ones enjoying the riches of the earth that they purport to be salvaging for all of us to enjoy. You see, in the end, the Russian revolution did not abolish class distinction; it simply created new ones.[9]

How does the proverbial wolf get access to a flock of sheep? He dons the coat of the sheep. Having done that, he can walk among them undetected, gaining their confidence by moving about without at first threatening any harm. When the right moment presents itself, the wolf strikes with a vengeance, carrying off as many sheep as he can and devouring them. When the sheep have forgotten the sordid incident, the wolf repeats the process, gaining their trust once again, and striking when he spies another one that he would like to have for dinner. The Democratic Party, often with Republican complicity, has been employing this tactic. With certainty, they have been duping the American public since the Progressive Era, encompassing the presidencies of Theodore Roosevelt, William Howard Taft, and Woodrow Wilson.

Although Teddy Roosevelt was a Republican, his cousin, Franklin Delano Roosevelt accused him of being a "closet Democrat." Taft was a Republican as well, but Woodrow Wilson, an avowed racist, was a Democrat. All three men, as you will see, implemented various planks of communism. The two Republicans focused primarily on government regulation of business, but Taft and Wilson dipped into the pockets of the average tax paying citizen. From the Progressive Era to this date, the intrusions into the lives of Americans by its government, largely led by Democrats, have simply grown in scale and scope.

This work is not about race, gender, social status, or class conflict. It is a work for all Americans, regardless of demographics, to read as a warning for the future. Utopian ideologies do not work. History is proof of that statement. In reality, utopias replace sensible government with dominant, tyrannical ones. They "strip the individual of his uniqueness," and they are inherently divisive notions, creating strife where none existed. By gradually imposing the precepts of Marxist utopianism on an unsuspecting population, they are like the wolf in disguise, and the people are led to believe the perfect society is just around the next bend in history.[10]

Table of Contents

Chapter One

MARCHING TO THE MARXIST ANTHEM

During the elections of 2008, 2012, and 2016, the Democratic Party, led by such figures as Barack Obama, the Clintons, both Bill and Hillary, and Bernie Sanders, began to use the word socialism more often than ever before. However, the electorate will recall, they still used it very sparingly lest somebody catch on to what they truly mean to say. In fact, there are millions of American voters who know exactly what they are saying, which helps explain one of many reasons why Hillary Clinton lost in 2016.

Those who vote for Democrats have bought into the notion that socialism and communism are two entirely different things because they choose to believe the official party line on the definitions, which is precisely what the leadership of the party wants everybody to believe, although Barack Obama is on record admitting there's little difference in communism and socialism.[1] The party elite must have hyperventilated when he made that admission.

In fact, socialism and communism are two very different words that look nothing alike, but they mean the same thing for all practical purposes. Webster says that socialism is a "theory advocating public ownership of means of production, with work and products shared alike."[2]

The same edition defines communism as "political theory demanding public ownership of economic resources."[3] Note the use of the common phrase "public ownership" in both definitions. "Means of production" and "economic resources" can be used interchangeably for they are inextricably one and the same.

Private ownership, or private enterprise, would denote ownership of businesses and means of production by individuals. In our economic system of capitalism there are literally millions of people from all stations of life who have ownership in multiple corporations through stock purchases and sales. Anybody can own a piece of any publicly traded corporation, a system that does a far better job of distributing wealth than the critics of capitalism will admit.[4] That is not the case in communism/socialism. Public ownership denotes possession by the state, or nation-state. Nobody but the state owns anything, including homes, land, cars, or any other type of property that a utopian state deems that individuals should not own. A fascist state is very similar to communism in most aspects other than ownership of the means of production. However, while allowing individuals to own factories or other means of production, the fascist state exercises extremely rigid controls over its operations.

Karl Marx and Friedrich Engels, coauthors of *The Communist Manifesto*, penned their outlandish doctrine in the middle of the 19th century when they became angry at the treatment of the working class as the modern world began to rapidly industrialize. Much of their rhetoric was scrawled onto the pages of *The Manifesto* with little thought as to whether or not they could prove it was a workable solution. It was written before health and safety regulations, pension plans, and company-sponsored insurance programs became the norm in the industrial world. By the middle of the 20th century workers were beginning to earn far better hourly wages than Marx and Engels would have imagined, and workers were beginning to get paid vacations and paid sick leave, among other benefits. All of these things became reality without the violent overthrow of governments, a mainstay of communist, or utopian, doctrine.

Meanwhile, the Russians put Marxism into practice under Vladimir Lenin, followed by Joseph Stalin. As enough time transpired, those ruthless dictators proved that socialism and communism were flawed political or economic systems. As the Union of Soviet Socialist Republics took shape, the middle class completely disappeared, replaced by something closely resembling serfdom. Workers, like pawns under the thumbs of the lords of the manors of medieval Europe, lost all of their rights in a system where the state owned the means of production. Even Russian farms failed under collectivization. In a three-year period alone in the 1930s, 7 million Russians starved to death as food crop production drastically declined under the weight of state ownership of the means of production.[5]

Today's Democratic Party in America does not want us to read *The Communist Manifesto*, nor do they want us to know the history of the world because that knowledge would open our eyes to the true plans they have for America. They want all of our property, and with it all of our rights. To get that, they have to destroy the middle class, just like Lenin and Stalin did. The middle class is a powerful economic force, and even more powerful at the ballot box, because they comprise the largest class of people in the United States, larger than the rich and poor combined.

Some Americans are afraid to read *The Manifesto* lest they be branded a communist. All of us need to read it, if for no other reason than to gain an understanding of just how ridiculous, yet dangerous, the ideology is to our political and economic freedoms. Thomas Jefferson set an example by reading the *Koran*, not because he was considering a conversion to Islam, but so he could better understand the enemy. In Jefferson's day that was the Barbary Pirates operating off the coast of Libya in the Mediterranean Sea. The pirates were Muslim, and Jefferson came to the conclusion that they believed the *Koran* gave them carte blanche to murder all nonbelievers and steal their possessions.[6] Socialism/communism, as posed by Marx and Engels, does exactly the same thing, just not in the name of religion.

Unfortunately for America's middle class we have lost our voice. Some believe the Democratic Party is the champion of the dispossessed. In reality, they want to concentrate all power in the hands of a few powerful figures. Others think the Republicans are going to save and support the middle class. Instead, the Republicans have often caved to the demands of the left-wing statists in Washington, allowing the government to assume powers it was never given by the Constitution.

Barack Obama, in opining that the powers of the president of the United States are too limited by the Constitution, was simply echoing the same sentiments as at least two of his predecessors in the White House, Woodrow Wilson and Franklin Delano Roosevelt. Wilson opposed the views of the likes of Charles de Montesquieu and John Locke on the natural rights of humans by espousing the ridiculous notion that rights are awarded by the government. He did not agree with the idea of checks and balances imposed on three branches of government, instead choosing to consolidate power in the executive branch.[7] FDR expressed contempt for limiting the powers of government, and in his "Second Bill of Rights" he went so far as to suggest that government should have the power to relieve people of their property "as the government sees fit." Of course, his Second Bill of Rights reads much like the ten planks of communism. FDR, usurping powers not allowed the executive office, basically began the deconstruction of the United States Constitution, initiating a "gradual revolution."[8]

The elite of the Democratic Party have bought into this socialist drivel to the point that they are willing to seize as much power as the unsuspecting electorate will allow them. They are statists in its purist form, and as I've pointed out in the introduction, the ideology closely parallels communism as implemented by Lenin in the Soviet Union. Internal conflicts arose where there had been none before,[9] much like what has occurred in the United States since the election of Barack Obama in 2008.

This exposé on *The Manifesto* will explore how Americans have been, and are continuing to be, duped by our leaders. And the statists/communists are slowly prevailing. Millionaires in Hollywood are supporting the movement with gusto, as long as the communists don't threaten their wealth. George Soros, an immigrant who never would have become as wealthy as he is if he had not been able to escape Nazi-occupied Bulgaria, is another example of the manifestation of communism. Soros has amassed a fortune in America, a net worth in the tens of billions of dollars, but he does not want the middle class to have anything. He wants to take as much from us as he can, and he knows full well which party to align with to get that done; the Democratic Party.

The Democratic Party continues to deny history. The Hollywood 10, they say, were not communists. All 10 of them held membership cards in the Communist Party, and all supported the violent overthrow of the United States government.[10] Today, the likes of Michael Moore, a high school dropout, George Clooney, Leonardo DiCaprio, Jane Fonda, and many other contemporary Hollywood "stars" are using their notoriety to perpetuate the cause of the Hollywood 10. However, all of them will howl the loudest if the government seizes their wealth. In other words, tax the middle class out of existence, but don't dare raise taxes on the wealth of Hollywood.

Democrats, in spite of their anti-Christian stance, will invoke the teachings of Jesus only when it suits their purposes, especially when discussing social and economic equality. As Richard Pipes points out, Jesus urged his followers to forsake possessions. However, communism grants government the power to seize one's possessions in the name of equality, making it fundamentally different from the lessons taught by Jesus whereby people can choose to willingly give their wealth to the dispossessed.[11] Economic equality and utopian pipe dreams, as espoused by Democrats, are fraught with peril. Utopias are starkly "regimented" societies where individuality and basic freedoms are destroyed, usurped by the state.[12]

What follows is a frightening essay on the true nature of the Democratic Party and why its ideologies are a danger to the civil liberties of all Americans regardless of race, religion, or social class. It spells the doom of America, the greatest democracy ever implemented in the history of the world in spite of its shortcomings, but so many Americans seem to be oblivious of the threat to their safety and freedom.

This is a must read for those at the poverty level. They will gain nothing by continuing to support a party bent on destroying America and its Constitution. While Democrats make promises to the poor when they want their votes, they turn their backs on them once in office. Even social programs, seemingly enacted to support those in need, are designed to keep the poor subservient to the state, not raise them to a new level in American society. By keeping them obligated and dependent on the false largesse of the Democratic Party, they ensure their undying loyalty and their votes. Otherwise, the party has no use for them.

Meanwhile, given time, we in the middle class will be forced to join those at the poverty level while the elite leaders of the Democratic Party continue their escalating attacks on the middle class. They intend to increasingly usurp powers never granted them by our Constitution and to steal the wealth of the nation. The wolf is among the sheep, luring them, in the words of Mark Levin, with "financial bribes in the form of entitlements."[13]

The Greek academic, Plato, defined a utopian state where the state reigns supreme over all else. In other words, Plato created a "totalitarian" state. This is the mantra of the modern liberal, or Progressive, or Democrat, and they are harkening back in time to Plato's *Republic*.[14]

Chapter Two

OLE HICKORY STEALS A FORTUNE

Andrew Jackson, arguably one of the angriest presidents in the entire history of the United States, with perhaps the exception of Donald Trump, was born into an impoverished family in March of 1767 in one of the Carolinas. How can that be, one might ask, a white man was born into poverty? Didn't Bernie Sanders tell us that whites don't know what poverty is like?[1] It's possible that Sanders meant to say that he and his ilk don't know what poverty is like, but no matter, because in the course of history lots of whites have been impoverished. The hills of West Virginia are teeming with whites struggling for survival, and have been for generations, but even more so since Obama gutted the coal industry. Thousands of white sharecroppers, and others who farmed the Oklahoma, Texas, and Kansas prairies, fled those environs for California during the Great Depression, many of whom found little or no work on the West coast. My grandfather was a tenant farmer in West Texas for several decades overlapping the Depression Era. My father and all of his brothers and sisters picked cotton on that hardscrabble farm every harvest season, no easy task for eight and ten-year-old kids. The family was most certainly poor. I'll bet Sanders never picked cotton.

But Old Hickory was not destined to remain a poor man, although the struggle would take him through his heroics in the Revolutionary War and the War of 1812, culminating in his political wars in the 1820s and

1830s. He was orphaned around the age of ten, not a pleasant situation for any child, so we can begin to feel some pity for him. However, he pulled himself up by his bootstraps, became self-educated, and earned a living in various ways, including Tom-thievery, setting the example for future Democrats.

Without doubt he was a leader worthy of accolades in both of the aforementioned wars, and became an astute politician, parlaying his hero status into political popularity by the time the 1820s rolled around. Little Andy also learned along the way that a politician can steal and get away with it, unlike bank robbers or purse snatchers who eventually are caught red-handed.

In 1824, reaching the peak of his political power, Andrew Jackson made his first run for president. All four candidates in that election, Jackson included, were representing the Democratic-Republican Party, the oldest political party in America as of that year, and a party that had outlived its major rival, the Federalist Party. In the early years of the Republic each party did not select a single representative to be placed on the ballot. In the election Jackson finished ahead of the other three men with 99 electoral votes. John Quincy Adams trailed him with 84 electoral votes, and William H. Crawford and Henry Clay garnished 41 and 37 votes respectively. If one does the math, they can readily see that Jackson only had 43.1% of the votes. To win the White House a candidate must have a majority, so this election was handed off to the United States House of Representatives.[2]

Henry Clay, although a westerner like Jackson, despised Andrew Jackson. Clay didn't much care for the other two either, but he knew that John Q. Adams, a northerner, was a supporter of his so-called American System, which included high tariffs to eliminate foreign competition in favor of American industry, continued support for a national bank, and government sponsored and financed internal improvements, especially in transportation systems such as roads, canals, and bridges. Jackson openly opposed a national bank.[3]

Henry Clay, desirous of a major role in the federal government, cut a deal that is often considered a corrupt one in the annals of American election politics. With the expectation that Adams would reward him with the Secretary of State post, Clay worked tirelessly to throw his support behind Adams for president, and the House ultimately voted for John Q. Adams.[4]

The already angry Jackson, who had struggled for survival most of his life, grew even angrier, not so much that the deal was dirty, but that he had been ganged up on by supporters of the other three candidates. Before the election of 1828, Andrew Jackson and others formed a new party, the Democratic Party, that would challenge the supremacy of the Democratic-Republicans. In part to avoid confusing them with this new party, the Democratic-Republicans changed their name to the National Republicans, and that party would eventually become extinct, just like the Federalists. The National Republicans were not the party of Abraham Lincoln, no more than the Democratic Party is the party of Thomas Jefferson.

Those in today's Democratic Party want to claim kinship to the old Democratic-Republicans, but only when it is expedient to win support for their socialist agenda. They are dreadfully wrong. The Democratic-Republicans opposed the idea of a large and intrusive government, and for the most part maintained a conservative interpretation, or strict constructionist view, of the Constitution. Any detailed and unbiased study of the history of America's political parties clarifies this assertion. Today's Democrats are the party of Andrew Jackson, whom you will shortly see is one of the most prolific thieves in American history, and many of his successors have mimicked his methods.

Democrats of today love to vilify Thomas Jefferson, a Democratic-Republican, because he was a slave owner. Most of them refuse to acknowledge Jefferson's proclivity to disparage the institution, but he lived in an era where many would not listen to him, or even listen to lukewarm abolitionists like Alexander Hamilton.[5] Although abolitionism can be traced to arguments posed at the constitutional convention, the movement did not take deep root until roughly 1820 with the arguments over the admission of Missouri as a slave state, and subsequently the passage of the Missouri Compromise. However, Democrats of today don't seem to have a problem with their founder and hero, Andrew Jackson, although he owned more than one hundred slaves and had no inclinations, as did Jefferson, to end the institution.

Hollywood and Democrats also attack Jefferson over his supposed relationship with Sally Hemings, a slave at Monticello, Jefferson's plantation in Virginia. A number of years ago, the film industry produced a movie for television with a black actress portraying Sally. She is described in histories as being very white, almost pale, with only a fraction of African blood. The film is a work of pure fiction, as there is absolutely no credible evidence that Jefferson carried on an amorous affair with Sally Hemings, but those who wish to destroy the Constitution must use every tactic to destroy Thomas Jefferson, who was instrumental in constructing the new government.[6]

Finally, the angry man, running as a Democrat, became president of the United States, winning both the elections of 1828 and 1832. He vetoed more bills than all of his predecessors combined, including rechartering of the national bank. The bank would die and not be revived again until the Progressive Era in the early 20th century.

Now that he was duly elected to the presidency, Old Hickory managed to perpetrate one of the biggest thefts in American history. Native Americans, especially descendants of those whose ancestors once resided east of the Mississippi River, have good reason to place Jackson at the top of their most despised white persons list.

Andrew Jackson had little trouble convincing the House and the Senate to sponsor a bill known most prominently as the Indian Removal Act of 1830. It was very easy for Jackson to convince Congress that it was in the best interests of the Natives that they no longer reside in their centuries old domiciles east of the Mississippi River. The so-called Five Civilized Tribes, Creek, Choctaw, Cherokee, Seminole, and Chickasaw, along with a number of other tribes had actually begun to live in increasing harmony with whites. In fact, many white men had married Indian women. However, conflicts still occurred, and Jackson used that as the rationale for his bill; but protecting Indians from white violence, and vice versa, was not the true purpose of the Removal Act. Andy lied, just like Democrats today continue to lie in order to steal.

The eastern Native Americans were resting comfortably on millions of acres of land that was coveted by thousands of whites, including the president of the United States. Jackson knew he could scrape together a fortune if that land were not occupied by its ancestral owners. The bill passed, Jackson signed it, then he had to try to convince Native Americans to leave of their own accord. The majority of them refused to acquiesce to the urgings of the president.

The angriest president in history then ordered the United States Army to round up Natives from north of the Ohio River, south into Louisiana, and east into Florida. They were forced out of their homes onto what history refers to as the Trail of Tears. It is not a single trail, although many of them would pass through places like Fort Smith, Arkansas, on their way to Oklahoma Territory, a region that Natives would begin to refer to as "The Nation." The exact number will never be known, but they died by the thousands of starvation, disease, and exposure. The Cherokee were among the last to be forced into the West, and suffered the hardest, with death estimates of 4,000 to 5,000, depending upon what source you are reading.[7]

Once the Natives were west of the Mississippi River, the rest was easy. Many whites, Jackson included, laid claim to some 30 million acres and converted it into cash by selling it off in parcels to other land-hungry whites who ventured up against the great river in increasing numbers. Andrew Jackson got his piece of the pie, thus the man born into poverty died a man of great wealth,[8] unlike Thomas Jefferson who died broke.

Karl Marx and Friedrich Engels did not publish *The Communist Manifesto* until 1848, three years after Andrew Jackson, the land thief, was laid into his grave. Nonetheless, the three men, Jackson, Marx, and Engels, could have easily identified with one another's methodologies. On the surface, all three men would appear to be the champions of the dispossessed or the oppressed. In Jackson's case, he was going to 'protect' Native Americans from being set upon by white settlers, and vice versa. In the instance of the two communists, they were the heroes of the working class who were suffering under the rigors of the industrial revolution.

Both approaches are cover stories for the "real McCoy." We have already examined Jackson's Tom-thievery, and his treatment of the Natives, which clearly shows there was never any anxieties about their security or safety. The result of Jackson's misguided "generosity" was thousands of miserable deaths on the trail into Oklahoma. The survivors did not enter paradise. They had to face the trials and tribulations of rebuilding their lives in a strange, and often inhospitable, environment. At least east of the

Mississippi they had occupied regions that were familiar to them. What did Jackson do for the survivors? Nothing, which is exactly what Lenin, Stalin, Mao, and other communist leaders in other states did for the survivors of their bloody rebellions. Old Hickory lived out the remainder of his life in comfort and ease on his beloved plantation, The Hermitage, in Tennessee, unconcerned about any Native American challenges to his security or safety.

Communism, as professed by Marx and Engels, works in similar fashion; convince the oppressed that their system will work. In other words, sell the lie, and then take everything from them.[9] Marx and Engels never intended for the oppressed working class to rise above its station in life. Their purpose was to create an all-powerful state that owned everything, including its subjugated people. To do that, one must keep the oppressed in their oppressed state, but dangle in front of them the proverbial carrot that will make them always think they are doing what is best for them. The state, after all, will make sure you have the basic needs of life; food, clothing, and shelter. In return, however, you must surrender an intangible human need, that of your freedom. By the reasoning of Marx and Engels, if the state grants you all of your material needs, then you owe your allegiance to the state, and only the state, and freedom is no longer a valid demand in the eyes of the despots.[10] In the end, the industrial workers in socialist states were treated much like the Native Americans were treated by Jackson, as a means to an end.

I suppose Andrew Jackson thought the Natives would love him for protecting them from the encroaching whites. He was wrong. Generations of Native Americans to this day have not forgotten the Trail of Tears. Meanwhile, Democrats since Andrew Jackson have continued, almost unchecked, their quest for absolute power, ownership of all lands and production facilities, including farms and ranches, and subjugation and impoverishment of the masses by an elite ruling class. Unfortunately for middle class Americans, the Republicans have either willingly or unwittingly, been a party to the creeping rise of communism in America.

What does this mean for the middle class? It means they have lost any true representation in our federal government. We are allowed to vote our choices, but voting seems to have boiled down to deciding which is the lesser of two evils; the statists/socialists/communists in the Democratic

Party,[11] or Republicans who turn their backs on the middle class as did George H. W. Bush when he raised our taxes in his one term in office. The founders of our nation railed against "taxation without representation," but the taxes they were being asked to pay were a pittance compared to what Americans pay today. In one sense those who are elected can claim they represent us, but once in office they often no longer listen to their constituencies.

We often hear the phrase "Democratic Socialism" as if the Democratic Party was supporting the most delightful political system in the history of the world. It is not, because democracy and socialism are inherently incompatible. Democracy is the manifestation of a free state of free-willed people. Socialism, as seen in Chapter 1, is communism. Both of them mean state control of every aspect of our lives; or statism. In *The Communist Manifesto*, both words, communism and socialism, are used interchangeably, and Marx and Engels proposed that all property be relegated to state control. Anybody who agrees with this nonsense doesn't understand that the ideology also entails the loss of freedom.

In the final analysis Marx and Engels' utopian worker's society is not what people may think. Equal distribution of wealth is not only impractical, it is impossible,[12] and the coauthors of *The Manifesto* misunderstood this or had no way of proving or disproving their theory. Their vision was a state in which nobody had anything, unless you were the ruling class, and the rulers would never give anything more to its subjects than what they thought they needed, including basic rights we have begun to take for granted, rights that are guaranteed by the Constitution of the United States.

Vladimir Lenin, who cared nothing for the poor, but instead sought revenge on a state that had tossed him into prison for a time, and executed his brother,[13] saw this clearly, and he implemented the ten planks of communism to the letter in what became the Union of Soviet Socialist Republics. Note the use of the word 'socialist' in the name of the new nation. Not a Communist Republic, but we all know it was a communist state. His successor, Joseph Stalin, one of the most brutal dictators in world history, simply took the relay baton upon Lenin's death and carried out the ruthless transition to communism accompanied by the ruin of Russia's industries and farms. But Joe Stalin always had plenty to eat, and a nice place to rest his evil mind and body. So did Andrew Jackson.

Subsequent chapters will explore how, and why, the Democratic Party has been pressing a communist agenda on Americans since Andrew Jackson. Again, he was no communist, but he certainly set a grand example of economic and racial oppression that will become the tools of the party he founded. Democrats have used those tools very subtly at times, and openly on occasion, convincing their followers that a worker's paradise, or Eden, or some other unattainable utopia is just over the horizon. America has been subjected to this mantra for more than 100 years. When will we tire of its hollow promises?

An example of the point I am making is as follows: When Barack Obama seized power in 2009, there were 38 million Americans living at the poverty level. By the time he left office in 2017, that number had soared to 46.2 million. How did the champion of the dispossessed manage to achieve this pseudo utopian goal? The answer is simple; he heavily increased taxes on the middle class, and many at the lower end of the middle class tumbled into poverty. The rest of us survived only because we were at somewhat higher levels to begin with. Obama, Hillary, Sanders, John Kerry, and many other Democrats firmly believe that the government has the right to take one hundred percent of our assets in the form of taxes. Given another term Obama would have grabbed even more of the wealth of the middle class. Had Hillary Clinton been elected, she would have carved up even more of the middle class's bank accounts.

Aristotle once said, "The worst form of inequality is to try to make unequal things equal." He was not speaking of racial equality or inequality, something our nation is familiar with, such as allowing African Americans to attend schools with whites. He was speaking of intellectual and economic equality. He is saying if a person chooses not to learn, then we cannot force them to, and if they choose not to work, we cannot force that on them either. Yet Democrats, who probably understand Aristotle, seem to defy his logic. As we work our way through the ten planks of communist/Marxist doctrine, we will see how Democrats use the word "equality," and many other tools such as fearmongering, as the means to achieve their true agenda; control of the masses and all of their wealth. There will never be complete social and economic equality, but Democrats will tell you it will be forced upon us. Aristotle, who was smarter than most Democrats, would disagree. In fact, he would say that we are destroying our democracy.

Chapter Three

OLD HICKORY DID IT, WE CAN TOO

The first plank of *The Manifesto* clearly illustrates that nobody, except the government, should own any property, and the government, and only the government, will dictate how land is used. Even as we continue the practice of private property ownership, our government is slowly and quietly increasing the volume of land under its control, either directly, or indirectly. Here's how Plank One reads: "Abolition of property in land and application of all rents of land to public purpose."[1]

This appalling proclamation of Marx and Engels awards all land, and any earnings from the land, to the government, and then the government will use it as they see fit. In the social upheaval of the 1960s, the counterculture movement argued this was the same concept Native Americans practiced when it came to property ownership. It is nothing of the sort. It is true that Native American concepts of land ownership differed greatly from that of Europeans in that they did not delineate property boundaries for individuals, and individual rights to protect their boundaries from trespassers. However, Natives would have found the notion that a government should own all of the land just as alien, and they did protect tribal boundaries from encroachment by other tribes. Natives had no governments, per se, but even their tribal councils would never profess that the land belonged only to the council, rather that it belonged to all of the people within their tribe and they could use it to the benefit of all. Marxism defies both the European concept of land ownership and the Native American concept.

Marx and Engels made it clear that the middle class is their target, although the majority of people constituting the middle class are not wealthy in the extreme, as is George Soros, a hero of Democrats at all levels. Communist doctrine states that "the middle class owner of property must be swept out of the way, and made impossible."[2] This statement is an admission that it is the middle class who will stand in the way of any attempts to implement communism. As stated before, the middle class in America is a huge percentage of the population, therefore it must be extinguished in order to suppress opposition to the most sinister goals of the Democratic Party. In other words, take everything from the middle class and relegate them to the same status as the poor, which does nothing for the poor constituents who seem to vote *en masse* for leftist policy makers.

The communist concept of land ownership is more akin to European feudalism, an era when the lord of the manor controlled vast tracts of land, but he allowed peasants to work the land as long as it was done in support of the manor. Vassals could be awarded use, but not ownership, of tracts of land called fiefs, but the vassal was required to do two things in return: first, produce goods for use on the manor; second, provide an army to defend the lord lest he be set upon by another lord, or sometimes by a vassal aspiring to become lord of the manor.

Were people free in this feudal political system? They were not. Peasants could be put to death in any number of hideous ways if they tried to escape from the manor. Vassals, too, were executed if they were deemed to be conspiring with other vassals to seize control of the manor.

The tyranny of manorialism and feudalism is one reason why there is no language in the Constitution of the United States granting property rights to the government, or the privilege of dictating what owners can or cannot do with their property. An argument from the radical leftists will be that Thomas Jefferson purchased Louisiana from France. That is true, but Jefferson never intended for the government to retain ownership of more than 800 million square miles of land, over 500 million acres. His primary purpose was to neutralize any renewed French threats in North America while gaining access to the port of New Orleans, but he intended for the land to be sold to settlers to use as they wished, then the government would use the proceeds of sales to retire the national debt. What a novel concept . . . retire the national debt!

However, since the publication of *The Manifesto* many presidents, mostly Democrats, but at least one Republican, have violated the Constitution by repeatedly claiming federal ownership of land, and dictating how one's private property may be utilized. Also, governments charge fees, usually in the form of taxes, for owning land or other property such as a home.

National Parks, et al

I enjoy the National Park system as much as anybody, and believe that land set aside for the enjoyment of the general population is not necessarily a bad idea, but that is still inherently an illegal confiscation of land by the government. The parks, though, are nice, and there's nothing blatantly wrong with the preservation of nature for the enjoyment of the general public.

However, a number of presidents have confiscated massive parcels of land that the vast majority of the general public will never see or use. All of these presidents have their rationale for doing so, but in truth they are practicing communism . . . "abolition of property in land." People cannot use it or own it if the government has seized it, and the government has no intention of ever allowing the public to use very much of the land with the exception of the relatively small amount of acreage designated as a 'park.' They cannot hunt, fish, or camp on the land. They cannot graze livestock or harvest minerals. One must ask why our government confiscates so much land which is never open to public use, or is not easily accessible to the average American.

Theodore Roosevelt placed more than 225 million acres under the protection of the National Forest Service, an agency also created during his administration. As stated in the previous paragraph, conservation is a good thing, but most of this land illegally set aside by Teddy Roosevelt, a Republican, but a Progressive Era Republican, is not under the auspices of the National Park System. Much of it lies unused, with the exception of relatively small tracts of land that have been used by several generations of ranching families for cattle, sheep, or horse grazing.

The purchase of Alaska by Secretary of State William Seward in 1867, and its subsequent and continued control by the federal government, is also illegal. If any government entity should own the land, the state of Alaska should be that entity, but that doesn't mesh with the Constitution either. In the 1970s, President Jimmy Carter (DEM), placed millions of acres of frozen tundra in northern Alaska (the ANWR) under federal protection from drilling operations, an activity that is proven to be environmentally safe, but Carter used environmental preservation as a pretext for his unconstitutional action.

Once again, the lord of the manor (Carter) dictated control and use of land that should be in the private domain. While the ANWR is, in theory at least, open to the public, none but a few hardy souls who can afford the equipment necessary to survive a foray into the Arctic National Wildlife Refuge will go there. It's not the same as venturing into Yellowstone National Park with the family for summer vacation. If one goes into the ANWR without proper gear, they will freeze to death in subzero temperatures within a matter of hours, if not faster. Or, they might become dinner for a polar bear, those cute, white, furry creatures with the "sad" faces because they are floating on an ice floe, something polar bears have done for a few thousand years. Those cute bears are huge, and it is a known fact that polar bears will stalk a human for days until the bear becomes hungry, then they will kill the human and eat him/her.

The wildlife in that nether region of the world would survive even an aggressive drilling program. But what most people do not know, and the leftists don't want us to know, is that only approximately 1/10th of the acreage is known to have oil reserves beneath it, reserves that could supply the world with much needed petroleum for another century. That means that 18 million acres would go untouched by exploration and drilling. Regardless of those facts, the point is that Carter violated the Constitution because it does not give the government the right to control use of that land, in much the same fashion that Andrew Jackson gained lordship over millions of acres of Native American land. Karl Marx and a handful of earlier philosophers were the only people who professed the notion that government should control all lands. Most recently, Barack Obama, another left-wing president and 'lord of the manor,' reinforced Carter's ban on drilling in the ANWR.

Barack Obama, incidentally, has the distinction of being the president who has confiscated more land in the name of preservation than any other in history. As a matter of fact, he snatched more than all other presidents combined, somewhere in the realm of 550 million acres, indicating that the Democratic Party is poised to step up their efforts to seize power and implement Plank One of communism to the fullest.[3] Before this leftist took office the amount of land under federal control stood at something near 390 million acres. Add the two figures together, and we are getting close to 1 billion acres "protected" by the federal government, or stolen by the government! One has to wonder what will happen once the government runs out of "public" land to confiscate. The next logical step would be to seize all private property, thus fully accomplishing the goal espoused by Marx in Plank One.

Or, perhaps, that step has already begun. When Harry Truman succeeded Franklin Roosevelt upon his death in 1945, the United States government was in possession of one-fourth of the economic assets of the country, including buildings, vehicles, and factories. More than 2 million people worked for the government, by far dwarfing the number of employees working for several of the largest corporations in America combined.[4] The numbers employed by the government have grown exponentially since the late 1940s as the government has increased the size of the staffs for senators and congressmen, added new, and often redundant, departments such as Homeland Security, and increased the size of existing departments. This is an alarming trend. The government is powerful enough to destroy us if that is what is deemed necessary to implement the Democratic Party's goal of statism. Karl Marx would be proud.

Native American Reservations

Why does the Bureau of Land Management control land that is designated as reservation land? If it is set aside for use by the Native Americans, then let them have it and leave them alone to enjoy it and use it as they choose. It was never the government's land to control in the first place. The BLM is an illegal organization, once again because there is no constitutional basis for its existence. Since its creation in the late 1880s, most of the actions of the BLM have done little, if anything, to benefit

Native Americans. In fact, their initial charge seemed to be to shrink the land available to Native Americans every time it was in the interests of whites. In reality, today's BLM is just another inefficient cog in the massive government bureaucracy, and we could reduce that expense by shutting them down. Native Americans who remain on reserve land would probably not miss them, nor would the tax payers, and Native Americans could use the land as they see fit without BLM intrusion. Other government departments could absorb the task of seeing that Native Americans receive benefits that have been designated for them.

Zoning Ordinances

Politicians, both Democrats and Republicans at local levels, are practicing statism, often without even realizing it or thinking about it. These would be mostly city and county governments spread across all fifty states, whether they are red states or blue states. Zoning ordinances established by city councils and county commissioners (parishes in some states) harken back to the medieval practice of feudalism. The lord of the manor tells a vassal he must produce wheat, or he must build a flour mill to support the manor. Present-day 'lords' tell property owners what they can and cannot build or operate on their private property . . . "application of all rents of land to public purpose." Cities, counties, and parishes exercise dominion over property that is supposed to belong to the person(s) who bought the property, whether it be a building or a lot.

If you are going to build a home on your property, local governments will not hesitate to dictate what size the house should be, and what materials of construction to use. You may want to build a wood-frame home, but they may say you cannot, it must be brick on at least three sides. One may argue that it is to preserve the aesthetic qualities of the zone in which it is being constructed. While that may be true, what gives anybody, especially governments, the power to dictate what one can do with their private property? Marx would agree with the mandated zoning rules, but for different reasons. He saw class structure in black and white terms, an elite ruling class with a mass of peasants beholden to them. Obviously, the peasants could not reside among the ruling class, thus spoiling their pristine environment. Zoning ordinances reduce the middle class to the same status as peasants in communist doctrine, and in medieval feudalism, not to mention, again, that they are not constitutional, although a 1921 Supreme Court decision ruled that zoning ordinances are constitutional.

We must rely on Supreme Court decisions to inform us about the constitutionality of laws and to provide a check on Congressional and Executive overreach when they pass a law that is not constitutional, but the Supreme Court is often subject to the whims of those seated on that august body at the time a law is reviewed. They are not always right. They do not become omniscient just because they put on a black robe, and they are not supposed to vote their individual opinions or feelings. Our Supreme Court has often voted decisions that do not mesh with constitutional reasoning, but even President Wilson (DEM) argued for the obstruction of the Constitution through the federal court system.[5]

A very good example of the biased nature of the Supreme Court is their approval of the segregation laws. In 1896, in *Plessy v. Ferguson*, the Supreme Court affirmed that segregation laws were constitutional as long as facilities for African Americans were equal to that of white facilities, invoking the so-called "separate but equal" doctrine. That landmark case would ensure that several generations of African Americans would be denied basic rights such as where they could eat, where they could sleep overnight when traveling, and what schools they could attend. Did the court, in 1896, issue a just and constitutional opinion in its ruling? An enlightened slate of Supreme Court justices, if "enlightened" is an appropriate term, overturned "separate but equal" in 1954 in *Brown v. Board of Education of Topeka, Kansas.* Basically, the court, in 1954, supported by the Constitution, ruled that the court in 1896 was wrong.

Having illustrated that the Supreme Court makes errors in judgment, it stands to reason that they were also wrong in 1921 when ruling that zoning ordinances were constitutional. If the men and women who wear the robes on our courts at any level believe they cannot err, then they are demigods. The Constitution does not support the decision reached in 1921.

Property Taxes, Etc.

How can one "pursue happiness" if the government begins to dictate what we can do on our own property, while at the same time taxing us for owning property? It is almost painful to be a property owner. Laws vary from state to state, but we are subjected collectively to an array of taxes; school, county, city, hospital districts, community college districts, and others, that not only encroach on our right to property, but prevent our "pursuit of happiness" in being a property owner. It is not surprising that the number of people who rent keeps growing as the various entities who govern the above-mentioned 'districts' seem to feel that they have carte blanche to freewheel with tax payer's money.

What gives any government entity the right to penalize us by taxing us for owning property? Locke would argue they don't have that right. Charles de Montesquieu agreed with Locke, stating that "excessive taxation and the confiscation of property" was "an assault on equality."[6] Our Constitution does not give governments the power to levy those "excessive" taxes. There are specific reasons that Congress can enact a tax, but a city or a county is not Congress.

School districts are among the worst at tapping the tax payer's bank accounts. Here's a hypothetical example: School district ABC has an elementary school building that is forty years old, and it has been deemed to be inadequate, or not conducive to good learning, or whatever other reason they can concoct to convince voters that they need (or want?) a new building. They place a referendum before the voters, meanwhile launching an advertising campaign favoring the bond issue by claiming that academic performance will rise as a result of the new building. The referendum passes, the tax payers are dunned for eternity for a building that is going to cost more than what the school board said it would, and the performance of the students does not shift upward. Sadly enough, academic performance continues to drop no matter how many new buildings we construct.

Why is it that Europeans are still able to learn in buildings that are 500 years old, but Americans have to have something new every three or four decades? Why is it that school district ABC could not maintain its building in good repair and cleanliness so that it continued to serve its function? It's a myth that new is always better.

Meanwhile, the tax payers suffer under heavy taxation that is now at 50% of our annual income, all taxes combined. None of this has to do with ethnicity. Whether the tax payer is African American, Hispanic, Native American, Asian American, or of European roots is not the argument.

People from all those ethnic groups, and more, make up today's middle class. It is obvious that our politicos are imposing these socialist ideologies on our nation's property owners and tax payers simply because we have allowed this Marxist mindset to invade our processes. We have become a society that believes the state knows best, and always has our best interests at heart.

- - -

Let's review Plank One of *The Communist Manifesto*: "Abolition of property in land and application of all rents of land to public purpose." Since the days of Andrew Jackson, the first Democrat to serve as president, the federal government has increasingly gained ownership of land. Today it's close to 1 billion acres!

Once the government has all of the land from border to border, then the ruling elite will have successfully eliminated the middle class, relegating them to the lower class, or a peasant class similar to European feudalism. Once that is accomplished, they will not have to play the Robin Hood charade any longer. We will have become serfs for life, and our children as well, and our grandchildren.

"Abolition of property in land." Barack Obama was the latest president to further implement this Marxist principle, placing hundreds of millions of acres under federal control, and dictating the use, or nonuse, of that land. Why does the government now have its thumb on 1 billion acres of land? What is the purpose of controlling so much? They cannot manage their own affairs in Washington, D. C.; how can they manage 1 billion acres of nature? The truth is that they cannot.

"Application of all rents of land to public purpose." The key word in that phrase is the word "public." The average person tends to think of it as meaning of benefit to all people, as in the general public. Nothing could be further from the truth. The public sector is the government. The private domain, or private sector, is the general populace. The government is not about to share its ill-gotten gains and wealth with the general public. Most of the 1 billion acres the federal government now controls are seldom, if ever, touched by humans, and all the rest of the land supposedly controlled by individuals has exorbitant taxes imposed on it by various levels of government ("application of all rents").

Perhaps the government is holding all of that unused land in abeyance for use by the ruling class at some point in the future, creating their own fiefdom or kingdom. Perhaps it is being held for something even more sinister, and the ultimate goal is to force all of us to live in government housing on government land assigned to us, unless you are one of the elite and already have a mansion erected on massive acreage you bought with tax payers' dollars, or seized outright.

The founders of the nation took their property rights ideals from men such as John Locke, a well-known 17th century philosopher. Locke's *Two Treatises on Government* relied on the notion that we are born into this world with certain "natural" rights, and these rights cannot be usurped by governments. One of the natural rights is property, and no one, including governments, "ought to harm" another's "possessions."[7] With certain limitations on how much property a person may acquire, Locke said we obtain property by the work, or labor, that we perform to make the property useful to society as a whole. We are not simply granted land without some effort in return. In other words, one may cultivate ten acres of some type of food crop, use what he needs for his family, and sell the surplus to others for their use.[8] But the property, in Locke's viewpoint, remains under the control of its owner, not of the state.

Locke lived well ahead of the rise of modern democracies, beginning with the United States in 1776, but nonetheless the founders of this country insisted on applying his ideals on property to the democratic process. Their interpretations of the philosopher are manifested in our Constitution, because they deliberately omitted any language that could be interpreted as public, or government, ownership of any land. People, not governments, should own the lands.

In writing the Declaration of Independence, Thomas Jefferson borrowed a phrase straight from Locke, but changed the reference to property. Instead of life, liberty, and property, Jefferson wrote, life, liberty, and the pursuit of happiness. Even Jefferson, who envisioned an agrarian society where everybody tilled at least some ground, perhaps recognized that not all persons would own property. In today's America, something close to half of all Americans rent their homes rather than buy them. In Jefferson's time, that number would have been much lower, but some were already tenants who paid the owner to live in their building or live on their land.

Andrew Jackson defied one of the main principles embedded in the Declaration of Independence when he stole property from Native Americans, therefore setting an example for his successors in the Democratic Party; Karl Marx, publishing his work only a few years after Jackson died, simply affirmed what Jackson had already put into practice.

Chapter Four

LET'S STEAL EVERYTHING

Plank Number 2 of *The Communist Manifesto* reads as follows: "A heavy progressive or graduated income tax."[1] Keep in mind that two angry men, Marx and Engels, wrote this drivel in the 1840s, when such a thing would have been considered very unusual.

At this point in world history, the 1840s, it is doubtful that there existed any type of systematic "income" tax statute anywhere in the world, although people had been taxed in varying forms, even before the days of the Roman Republic. Usually, the taxes were paid on goods produced, utilizing a somewhat arbitrary method of calculating and imposing the taxes. Farmers in the Roman Republic and Roman Empire did, in fact, suffer from heavy taxation in order for Rome to pay for its numerous wars of conquest, build magnificent structures such as the Coliseum and Circus Maximus, and keep emperors and their extended families living in lavish surroundings and lifestyles. Those farmers rebelled, but the might of Rome would usually crush the revolts in due time.[2] In truth, the taxes Rome imposed on its farmers would be mere pocket change in comparison to what Americans are being forced to pay today.

Marx said that governments could basically take all of the wealth of the bourgeoisie, and that would lead to an equal distribution of wealth and elimination of social classes.[3] He was wrong again. In reality it leads to a powerful, despotic, totalitarian government ruling over a mass of people with nothing. It turns the government into legal pirates where "plunder becomes a right."[4] In the name of "extreme equality," Democrats impose increasing levels of taxation on America's taxpayers which is leading to increasing levels of inequality and "despotism."[5] The Democratic Party in the United States is striving to achieve that goal. But they have had, and still do have, plenty of accomplices in the Republican Party. Abraham Lincoln, although prone to disregard the Constitution as well when it suited his purposes, would shed tears of sorrow at the way his party, by inaction or downright duplicity, allows Democrats to pilfer the wealth of the nation.

Taxation in Early America

In the early days of the American Republic, the country operated under the Articles of Confederation, a government body that actually feared imposing taxes lest they be cast in the same light as old King George III and British Parliament had been in the days leading up to the Revolution. The Articles were the opposite extreme of heavy taxation, and it left the fledgling nation bereft of sufficient operating funds. The government could barely maintain an army for its defense, and lack of funds became a major reason why the founders revised the structure of the government, culminating in the adoption of our Constitution.[6]

In Article I of the Constitution, the framers created a bicameral legislative body composed of the Senate and the House of Representatives. The old Articles of Confederation consisted of a unicameral legislature with no executive office or federal court system. We refer to the bicameral legislature as Congress, and in Section 8 of Article I, the authors spelled out the duties of Congress, including to "collect Taxes, Duties, Imposts and Excises."

The new Congress now had explicit powers to impose taxes, but even they were very reluctant. However, Alexander Hamilton convinced both houses of Congress and the nation's first president, George Washington, to impose not only a tariff, or duty, on imports, but also a tax on whiskey manufactured by farmers. As stated earlier, the leaders of the nation feared imposing taxes because they felt they might incite rebellion. They were right. Hamilton's whiskey tax outraged the farmers in western Pennsylvania, who were manufacturing the alcoholic beverage to supplement their meager earnings from agricultural pursuits. But the new government wielded its power, eventually forcing the protestors to back down.[7] Under President Jefferson, the tax was repealed. The whiskey tax, to iterate, was pocket change compared to what Americans face today, yet it raised the hackles of those most impacted by the tax. Hamilton, to be fair, was simply trying to retire debts accrued by individual states during the Revolution, and certainly had no intention of taking one hundred percent of anybody's annual earnings.

It was during the American Civil War that the United States, the Union (North), passed the first income tax in the nation's history and created the Internal Revenue Bureau.[8] Wars are expensive to prosecute, to say the least, and the Civil War was extremely costly for both the Union and the Confederate States of America. Abraham Lincoln fully supported the use of an income tax to defray some of the cost of the war for the North, but the bulk of the costs were covered by the sale of war bonds, and the income tax was never meant to be permanent. It was simply a wartime measure. The Confederacy, harkening back to the days of the Revolution and the tax revolts, were loath to pass an income tax, instead they imposed a tax on individual states.

Nonetheless, the measure was one of several imposed by Lincoln's administration that was illegal from a constitutional standpoint. He also jailed key members of Maryland's state government without habeas corpus in order to forestall a secessionist vote in that very important border state. Lawmakers, since the adoption of the Constitution, understood that income taxes were taboo. Congress could levy taxes on imports and exports and on the production of goods as they deemed necessary, but a person's hard-earned salaries and wages were sacrosanct. Personal income was property, and Congress could not take one's property without due process according to the Constitution. Due process does not entail taxing a person's income with reckless abandon.

In the spirit of Andrew Jackson, a thief by any definition, in the late 1800s, a small-potatoes operator in Montana by the name of Johnny Healey, the sheriff of Choteau County and a Democrat, levied his own set of local taxes on constituents in his bailiwick. Healey was operating a "ring" much like the Democratic Party "machines" in major cities back east, and his taxes were only imposed on non-democrats, then the spoils were divided among his cronies, all of whom were powerful Democrats in Choteau County, Montana.[9] In the late 1800s and early 1900s, Jim Pendergast, also a Democrat, built a small empire in Kansas City, Missouri, by stealing from the city coffers and rigging elections in his favor.[10]

Progressivism

The Progressive Era, as it is called in American history, roughly includes the administrations of three presidents, Theodore Roosevelt and William Howard Taft, both of them Republicans, and Woodrow Wilson, a Democrat. Parts and pieces of Progressivism were embraced by both political parties, especially when it came to the growth of government and its oversight of American industry. We have already seen how Teddy Roosevelt created the National Forest Service as well as the National Conservation Commission. But he also created the Pure Food and Drug Administration to police real or imagined improprieties in the food and drug industry, including meat packing plants, and he attacked a number of corporations that were deemed to be monopolies. Other government agencies created during the period, or close to it, were the Interstate Commerce Commission and the Federal Trade Commission, both intended to prevent monopolies in industry. Coupled with the revival of the national bank, the Federal Reserve System was created to give the federal government power over the banking industry. Thus, we have the early stages of massive government control of industry.

Journalists of the Progressive Era, known as "muckrakers," the worker charged with cleaning the muck out of horse stables, were a driving force influencing the growth of government, but much of their work was exaggerated in the form of what was known as "yellow journalism," sensationalizing of stories in order to increase newspaper sales. It is important to note that increased sales was the end game for the muckrakers, whether or not their work did much to improve the lives of Americans. Many of the muckrakers, such as Theodore Dreiser, Jacob Riis, and Lincoln Steffens, were strong supporters of socialism, a.k.a. communism, and their book-length works reflected Marxist ideals in hopes of undermining American democracy.

As the government grew, so did the need for revenue to pay for all those new agencies, and it did not stop with the end of the Progressive

Era. However, it was the Progressives during the presidency of William Howard Taft (REP) who recognized that there was a huge economic resource in America that had not been tapped but once since the Civil War . . . personal income. The earlier attempt to impose an income tax had been struck down by the courts who viewed the measure as unconstitutional,[11] therefore, Progressives, who were the forerunners of the great liars in politics, hid a permanent income tax amendment in a tariff bill in 1909.[12] The bill passed in 1910, but the amendment itself still had to be ratified. Surprisingly, state after state ratified a measure that the high court had deemed illegal, dooming their personal income to eternal taxation, and the 16th Amendment, a permanent income tax, became part of our Constitution in the final months of Taft's only term in office.

It is important to emphasize that Congress could not legally tax income because the highest court in the land had already said it was unconstitutional to do so. With the highest court in the land posing an obstacle, it became imperative that the Progressives amend the Constitution in order to legitimize an act of Congress that the founders had deliberately omitted from the powers granted to Congress. It is unfortunate that the amendment was not repealed in its infancy because we have been forever saddled with federal, state, and local governments which are running amuck with taxation with representation; in other words, practicing communism . . . "a heavy income tax."

The ink had barely dried on the page where the 16th Amendment had been added to the Constitution when Progressive lawmakers, supported by Woodrow Wilson (DEM), once again hoodwinked the public. They buried a graduated income tax within the pages of the Underwood Tariff Bill, thus making complete the institution of Plank 2 of communism. Barack Obama employed this trick very well, hiding huge tax increases on the middle class within the 2,000 or so pages of the Affordable Care Act, hereinafter referred to as the (un)Affordable Care Act or the Abominable Care Act.

Proponents of a graduated income tax repeatedly argue that a flat tax is more burdensome on the lower-income classes. That argument has little or no merit, because people at the poverty level pay no income tax at all, and the lower middle class pays very little. As a matter of fact, many in those income classes take advantage of what is called the Earned Income

Credit, a tax law passed under Ronald Reagan that allows them to recover 100 percent of what was deducted from their paychecks throughout the year, plus a calculated sum based on earned income. In other words, they get a tax refund greater than the amount they paid in the course of a year. On the other hand, one can argue that a graduated tax is unfair to those who have worked hard to improve their financial position, as many Americans still do, although in decreasing numbers. Those at the peak of the tax structure today, the upper class, the wealthy, or whatever term you choose to refer to them, already pay 58.7% of the taxes collected by the Internal Revenue Service.[13] The rest of us, comprised of the vast majority of Americans, pick up the other 41.3% of taxes collected annually.

The basic argument remains that income taxes are illegal because the founders were protecting that asset in the Constitution by not explicitly granting Congress the power to tax income. This assertion is supported by the Supreme Court's decision prior to passage of the 16th Amendment. Compounding the issue is the way that our government under Taft and Wilson sneakily pushed both the 16th amendment and the graduated income tax past the public by hiding them in other bills, a dastardly and dishonest act of deception by elected officials and a betrayal of their fellow Americans. It's the same thing as a person selling a car with 25,000 miles on it, but first rolling the odometer back to zero, and passing it off as a brand-new car. I assure you that that is an illegal practice. Everybody who voted for the 16th Amendment and the graduated income tax should have been jailed and/or fined for their dishonesty, along with those who voted for the (un)Affordable Care Act, which is one of the biggest tax heists of all time perpetrated on the American middle class tax payers. Even the Supreme Court of the United States called the (un)Affordable Care Act a tax bill.[14]

The Carrot and the Mule

Let me draw a mental picture that many people are very familiar with anyway. You have a cart and a mule, and you would like to hitch the mule to the cart so it can pull the cart containing something you wish to move from Point A to Point B. But the mule is stubborn and will only stand still. You concoct a solution to get the mule to move. You hang a carrot from the end of a stick short enough to dangle it in front of the mule's eyes, but long enough that the carrot is just out of reach of the salivating mule. Also, you put blinders on the mule so he can only see the carrot, and not much of his surroundings. When the mule develops a desire to eat the carrot, he begins to walk toward it, but the stick holding the carrot is either attached to the cart or is being held by a person seated in the cart. As the mule moves, so does the cart and so does the carrot. The idea is that the mule will continue to walk forward in order to get to the carrot while the carrot continues to move at the same pace. Thus, the poor mule will never reach the elusive, dangling carrot, but he will eventually deliver his cartload to Point B. This is precisely how Democrats, and sometimes Republicans, treat lower- and middle-class Americans.

In the mid-1800s, political "machines" seized control of the governments of almost every major city in America, especially the northern cities. They have been applying the carrot trick on the lower and middle classes for close to two centuries now, an idea that in reality embodies the concepts of Karl Marx. The "machine," such as Tammany Hall in New York City, would steal millions from the city's coffers by forcing them to accept contracts with selected companies, pad the bid for whatever job they were going to do, and divide the stolen profits among themselves. To win over the downtrodden element of the city, thus ensuring they will vote for the "right" politicians, the "machine" operates as if it's a modern-day Robin Hood, stealing from the rich and giving to the poor. However, the lower classes remain the lower classes because they never get enough of the loot (the carrot), and they never will. The "machine" takes the lion's share. That is by design. It stands to reason that they cannot allow the dispossessed to become middle class while they are busy stealing all they can get from the middle class, plus they would lose an important block of votes.

George Parr, from Duval County, Texas, operated in a similar fashion in numerous counties in South Texas for several decades. Hispanics loved the man because he would fork over a few bucks for groceries from time to time, or he would help with an especially burdensome medical expense. However, in return for the handful of dollars Parr passed around, they would have to vote for candidates for public office according to his wishes, and he would usually know how they voted. But those in the lower economic levels in South Texas remained there. Parr would not allow them to rise in stature economically because he would lose his voter base if that happened. He kept that carrot constantly moving.

Meanwhile, Parr orchestrated one of the most crooked elections in our nation's history, sending Lyndon Johnson to the Senate by using the votes of dead people in an extremely close election. In the senatorial election of 1948, the infamous Box 13 from Alice, Texas, in Jim Wells County, was the last precinct in the entire state to report in, and the voter rolls, according to some who saw them, were filled with dead people who voted in alphabetical order, all of them for Lyndon Johnson. Of course, George Parr, LBJ, and all of their henchmen were Democrats.[15]

The Abominable Care Act, or the (un)Affordable Care Act, or Obamacare, or whatever you choose to call it, is "machine" politics on the grandest of scales. It would not have passed muster in the Supreme Court if the Court had not called it what it is, a tax bill, and Congress can levy taxes; therefore, it was deemed constitutional, even though we know that income taxes are unconstitutional. However, the (un)Affordable Care Act was an underhanded, sleazy, dastardly move to bilk the middle class out of its hard-earned dollars. Did the folks at the poverty level benefit? As stated previously, the number of people living at the poverty level climbed by 8.2 million during the reign of the socialist president and his cohorts in the Democratic Party.

All middle class retirees who had a company-sponsored health insurance plan saw their premiums more than double due to taxes on their insurance carriers. Private health insurance premiums rose for everybody who had health insurance, and Obamacare is too expensive for most people. The Abominable Care Act pushed middle class taxpayers into higher income tax brackets, proof that it was nothing more than a tax heist. Taxable earnings also increased because itemized deductions for health insurance premiums were eliminated, forcing those who were able to itemize deductions to pay tax on more of their hard-earned income. The loss of these tax advantages caused a precipitate decline in home ownership. The so-called "fine" that one pays if they don't have health insurance would be illegal had the Supreme Court not called it a tax as well. It's nothing less than a punitive measure applied to those who cannot afford insurance premiums, including Abominable Care. Paying a fine suggests criminality, so Obama has basically made criminals of millions of people without habeas corpus, a clear violation of the Constitution. However, the Supreme Court carefully avoided using the word "fine," instead, they called the mandate a tax. Meanwhile, the costs of health care have climbed along with the price of prescription medicines. Whatever became of "hope?" It was just a word to rally the votes.

Obama's thrust into our pockets was by design. The feint (the carrot) was that it would give health care insurance to those without it, but the reality is that it was to illegally take more property from the middle class; just like what the machines did by handing out a few bucks on election day, or distributing loaves of bread a couple of times a year. In the end, the poor are still the poor, and the middle class are rapidly joining them. Just for clarification, the political machines in the major cities were always Democrats. Obama knows this. He has lived in one of the most corrupt cities in America; Chicago, Illinois. He is well-versed in underhanded politics, as well as deceptive and manipulative tactics.[16] Democrats in the House and the Senate who voted for his Abominable Care Act never read the document. It was, by design, too cumbersome to read in its entirety.

Where does all the money that is being confiscated by Obamacare go? We don't really know, but I assure you that the folks who were impoverished when Obama took his first oath of office are still impoverished. The carrot has kept moving. We do know a couple of billion went to Iran, a nation who hated us before they got the money, and has continued to hate us since. It certainly does not provide more health coverage unless you choose to believe the lie that 20 million people are on Obamacare. Democrats will not admit that about 24 million people lost their health insurance in the aftermath of passage of the (un)affordable Care Act. We also know that Obama bought a $1.5 million yacht in his retirement. The Clintons are enjoying a second fortune they amassed while Obama was president. Just good old-fashioned Democratic Party machine politics. Steal what you can while you can. In the final analysis, Obamacare was intended to tax the middle class while centralizing control of the health care industry in the hands of the state, not truly for the purpose of giving everybody universal, affordable health care.[17]

Meanwhile, what are the Republicans doing about the (un)Affordable Care Act? As of this writing, Donald Trump has been in office more than a year, and efforts to repeal Obama's signature bill appear to be feeble at best.

While Democrats continue to practice Tom-thievery and Tom-foolery with the money rolling in from Obamacare taxes, Republicans duck for cover lest they be branded a racist, or be accused of being insensitive to the needs of the poor. They have been told a new lie; millions will lose their health insurance if the Abominable Care Act is repealed and/or replaced. I recall being warned that's what would happen if Obamacare passed. It did happen, but Democrats didn't care, and the liberal press will never admit that millions lost their health insurance. Meanwhile, Republicans are turning their backs on their constituents.

Democrats are wolves in sheep's clothing. Using words like socialist or progressive, they appear to be the party of the dispossessed. In reality, they are true communists, or statists, and will continue on that path until all ten planks of communism have reached fruition. Russia has to be laughing at us, because they know what lies ahead. They went through the process in a more brutal and acute sense, but the United States is on that brutal path now. The Democratic Party once was much more subtle with the process, thus the term Democratic Socialism, or one could say, Democratic Communism. But subtleties are dropping away as evidenced by the violence perpetrated by crowds before and since Trump took office. Look at the ravings of Hollywood figures like Ashley Judd, who was so "outraged." I, too, am outraged that Democrats pretend to be the only ones fit to rule even as they are stealing our wealth, practicing communism with gusto. Where is Aristotle when we need him? Republicans are not much help.

Social Security

I often wonder if, perhaps, President Franklin D. Roosevelt developed the idea for Social Security from Charles Ponzi. Ponzi took millions from people in the early 1900s, promising them huge returns on their investments. In reality, he simply transferred money from one person's account into that of another's in order to make it appear they were earning big bucks. Charles Ponzi was the only one earning big bucks. I can almost imagine the thoughts running through FDR's head. "Let's tell the American people another lie. After all, they'll never figure it out." Both Hillary Clinton and Barack Obama are on record as possessing the notion that Americans are stupid. How many times in eight years did we hear

Obama say, "What the American people NEED to understand?" That comment, oft-repeated by the narcissist, is an indication that he thought us ignorant peasants, and he was the brilliant mind come to rescue us from our imbecility.

Let's return to FDR. I can imagine him saying in private, "Let's tell them we're going to take a small piece of their money each year and hold it as a retirement income. But we've got to keep voters coming to the polls to vote for us, so we'll slip just a little of it out of the government coffers each year and hand it to people who never earned it, much less paid it. The ignorant sods will never know."

Mr. Roosevelt, I know. I walked into a social security office in Corpus Christi about three years ago and was appalled to see about 150 people waiting to file claims. Almost all of them were half my age or younger. I was approaching 65, and I began to wonder what these people did to earn my money. I know that many of them never paid a dime into Social Security. Then I thought how nice it would have been to retire at 35, lay on the couch, drink beer and watch television while working people continued to pay me to do nothing. I scanned the crowd in search of those who might be there to claim disability. I could not find even one who remotely appeared to be disabled, and I stormed out in anger, thinking of all the years I had spent working hard and being forced to pay into a system that the government lied about.

Recently I was in a conversation with an older gentleman in a museum in Kansas. The man said to me, "The Democrats 'gave' us social security, and they 'gave' us Medicare. What have the Republicans ever 'given' us?" It would have been useless to argue the point with the man, so I simply let it pass in silence, but my thoughts were that Democrats did not give us those things. They forced us to pay for them our entire life. Just take a look at your pay stub and you'll see the deductions for both of those programs. We pay for them! They are not free! Again, like Ms. Judd, I am outraged, but for a different reason than she was so inflamed. I am outraged by those who think those programs are free.

Social Security passed during the Great Depression, an era when the country was very vulnerable. I am sure that it seemed like a great idea to most people in an era when almost none had any kind of retirement income to look forward to, and twenty-five percent of the nation was unemployed.

But Democratic Party politics duped all those people. When they started deducting the money from people's wages, the government failed to inform them that as soon as they got their hands on the money, they were going to hand it out to those who would vote for Democrats. Would they hand out enough to make them rich? Hell no, they would only hand out enough to make them think the Democratic Party was their friend; remember the carrot and the mule?

For more than two decades now, we have been hearing that Social Security is going broke. The only way it can go broke is to pay out more than it takes in. The only way that can happen is to hand out money to millions who never contributed, or to funnel the Social Security funds into all kinds of other pork belly schemes of the Democratic Party, an act similar to what Ponzi did with his investors. Ponzi was the pork belly. Did Charles Ponzi go to prison? Yes, he did. By that rationale, all Congressmen and Senators who voted for using Social Security funds to further their own agendas, and any president who signed such bills should belong in prison. They have stolen from the taxpayers with a promise to treat the money as a retirement fund, and then abused the taxpayers' investment.

For the record, Barack Obama let a reduction in Social Security deductions from the George W. Bush era come to an end, raising what we pay into the system without the stroke of a pen. Why? Because he and his henchmen were pilfering social security funds for Democratic Party agendas, but he also understood all too well that it dovetailed nicely with Marxist doctrine; let's take it all from the American people. "What the American people need to understand" is that one day they will have nothing. Once again, I am compelled to warn those at the poverty level that it will include them as well. The entire middle class will simply join you, while the Democratic Party elite and its supporters will control everything. At that point, there will no longer be a need for the carrot, and our freedoms will have evaporated.[18]

Gasoline Taxes, Sin Taxes, and Other Tom-Thievery

Most Americans know how much they pay in sales taxes on goods purchased in almost any retail establishment. In Texas, it runs near 8.25

%. However, what many do not realize is that the taxes, especially federal taxes, on gasoline, tobacco, and alcohol are much higher. Taxes on gasoline currently run near 80 cents per gallon. Current gasoline prices are hovering near $2.25 per gallon in the region where I currently reside. That means we are paying a 35% tax on fuel, nearly four times the rate of sales tax that we pay on most other products.

One argument for the exorbitant tax on fuels is that it's designed to reduce our reliance on hydrocarbon fuels. This is not the real reason. It's simply one more way to rob Americans, and pad government coffers. The argument for the so-called sin taxes on tobacco and alcohol products is that they will create healthier Americans by forcing them to quit smoking and consuming alcoholic beverages. The argument is a big lie, and since when did the Constitution give the federal government the rights to be guardians of our health? Many of the people who continue to smoke and consume alcohol in large quantities tend to be at lower income levels, people who really cannot afford to spend their earnings on such wasteful pursuits, therefore the federal government is heaping an extremely exorbitant tax on the poor, contradicting their argument against a flat-rate income tax.

The cold, hard truth is that the politicians who keep raising these kinds of taxes are not all that interested in our health. They just want our money. Over the past decade, there has often been talk of heavily taxing sodas, or placing limits on the size of soda drinks that can be sold in fast-food chains and convenience stores. Without a doubt, that would be unconstitutional. If I want to gulp down five gallons of soda every day, that's none of the government's business. They have no right to stop me. For the record, I don't plan to drink that much soda, but I'm simply making the case that the government has no right to interfere in our lives to that degree.

Taxing the middle class out of existence is the mantra of the Democratic Party, which falls neatly in line with Marxism. Those who support this movement believe the state will see to our every need, including our health. They are being duped by liars and thieves.

Chapter Five

YOU'RE DEAD, IT'S ALL MINE NOW

One of the most ludicrous of Karl Marx and Friedrich Engels' economic and political notions concerns that of the right of inheritance. Plank 3 of *The Manifesto* says, "Abolition of all right of inheritance."[1] Those two communists agreed that "this person [the bourgeois, the upper-middle class entrepreneurs] must be swept out of the way, and made impossible."[2] In other words, the upper-middle class must certainly be destroyed. But don't touch the upper class, especially if they hold all of the power, which makes it easy to conclude that class differences would not disappear simply because the middle class disappears. There will simply be two classes instead of three, the ruling elite and a mass of peasants, a return to the medieval practice of feudalism.

It is true that all Democrats from the Progressive Era to Jimmy Carter did oppose the spread of communism. To understand this phenomenon, we have to explore the real reason they seemed to be anticommunist. Was it because they opposed the economic concepts of Marx? Not entirely. Then why would they bother? Suppose the Soviet Union had succeeded in bringing down the United States during the Cold War instead of what finally happened. Who would have been the ruling elite? Obviously, the Soviets, the Politburo, the Communist Party of the USSR, not Americans, would have run roughshod over the world. The Democratic Party doesn't want that. They want to be the ruling elite!

There are those who deny that there was ever a movement in the United States to topple the government, replacing it with a utopian socialist system; in other words, communism. As early as the 1920s, the Comintern, a Soviet organization bent on spreading communist dominance, was infiltrating the growing film industry in the United States, as well as all of the major labor unions. Their charge was to foment anarchy with the purpose of taking over the government in the midst of chaos. Historians prefer to ridicule this fact by referring to it as the First Red Scare, the moniker suggesting that the activities of the Comintern were nonexistent. There were plenty of Americans who were aiding and abetting the Comintern, and Democrats greatly feared the loss of their power if the infiltrators succeeded when the USSR was in a position to seize power in the Western Hemisphere.

In 1916, only three years after the establishment of the 16th Amendment allowing the federal government to "legally" tax personal income, Congress slipped another bill by Americans in order to also tax one's inheritance. Keep in mind this was still in the Progressive Era and the president who signed this early law on inheritance taxes was Woodrow Wilson, a Democrat. By the way, he remains a hero of Democrats, in spite of the fact that he was an avowed racist who professed that *The Birth of a Nation*, a silent film, was his favorite movie. That film glorified the Ku Klux Klan as a patriotic organization, and it's no surprise that it was released in 1915, a mere 20 years after the Supreme Court of the United States decided that "separate but equal" facilities were legal and constitutional, condemning several generations of African Americans to sub-standard education as well as numerous other socially demeaning activities.

Woodrow Wilson would have agreed with the man who just left the White House, Barack Obama. In 2012, Obama, while campaigning for his second round of Tom-thievery, said, "If you've got a business, you didn't build it. Somebody else made that happen."[3] This idea, which smacks of absurdity, sums up Obama's Marxist leanings in two brief sentences. Entrepreneurship is not real, nobody worked hard to build a profitable business, it simply happened because of "somebody else." The very hallmark that built America was being ridiculed by the president of the United States. I have to wonder if he would apply the same concept to the political machines. Did they build the organizations that stole millions from taxpayers, or did somebody else do that for them? The obvious answer is that the machines were built by the men who operated them, just like people built businesses.

In the early 1900s, an African American woman named Sarah Breedlove, who came to be commonly known as Madam C. J. Walker after she married, utilized her business acumen to develop a cosmetics empire as well as a chain of beauty parlors in Chicago. By 1915, Sarah Breedlove was the wealthiest black woman in the United States, and quite possibly the first African American and female self-made millionaire.[4] One must wonder if Barack Obama and other Democrats would apply their flawed logic to Breedlove's small empire. Would they tell her, were she still alive today, that "somebody else made it happen?" The very notion that Sarah Breedlove didn't build her business is an idea that is so absurd it defies all logic.

This is the same kind of warped logic Marx applied in Plank 3. He was basically saying that any assets accrued by a person in the course of their lifetime didn't truly belong to them, therefore it goes "back" to the state when they die. Currently, inheritance taxes do not take everything, but Democrats will never give up until they can wrest complete control of inheritances at every level of the economic spectrum. In 2015, Obama made an attempt to reach deep into estates left behind by death. He lied in his campaign in 2012, stating that he would not hit middle class families with increased estate taxes. No true believer that the state is our greatest benefactor is going to leave the middle class alone, especially since Marx and Engels identified the middle class as the enemy of statism. They are considered by Democrats as the evil ones, the ones that drive capitalism, but the truth is that Democrats fear the voting power of the middle class. In the second to last full year of his second term, when he figured all had forgotten his hollow campaign promise to not attack the financial assets of the middle class, Obama went after them with a vengeance.[5] When the Republican controlled House of Representatives voted down his atrocious estate tax bill, Obama struck back with his usual remarks about how Republicans in the House of Representatives were only protecting the rich. He could not admit that they were protecting the middle class.[6] But I suppose that he believes that hourly wage earners who are middle class are really rich people like him and his cronies in the Democratic Party.

If one analyzes Marxist doctrine on inheritance taxes, along with Marxist notions on the elimination of the middle class, it is easy to understand why Democrats, of late Obama, the Clintons, Bernie Sanders (an Independent who ran for the Democratic nomination in 2016), and many others, propose such sweeping attacks on the middle class. It would be very informative if we could have both Marx and Engels sit on a talk show today and explain Plank 3. As it turns out, Friedrich Engels and Karl Marx never put in an honest day's work in their lives. Then what sustained them? How did they obtain food, clothing, and shelter? Did they sleep under bridges and beg for food? Actually, they lived quite comfortably, supported by the INHERITANCE passed down to Mr. Engels, whose family were capitalists, heavily into the textile industry.[7] I wonder how the two Deans of Dimwits would rationalize Plank 3 while living off the proceeds of the very thing they wanted to take from the middle class.

I am familiar with a family whose last surviving parent recently passed away. Each of the surviving children received a grand sum of slightly over $3,000 from the estate. None of them were made rich by this sum, but none of them whined about it either. Would you believe that Democrats, especially those in power, think that that money belongs to the government? Their parents, according to Marxist theory and Obama's irrational argument, did not earn the money through hard work, diligence, and perseverance. In communist doctrine, somebody else put the wheels in motion that put the money in the parents' bank accounts. Marx and Engels believed that all earnings emanate from the state, thus should return to the state. An easy thing to say for two people who never really worked for their sustenance.

Most politicians have no clue what it's like to toil eight or more hours per day in boiling sun, or freezing temperatures, or driving rain, or dust storms, or sleet, or any other outdoor conditions. They have no idea what it's like to work so hard that every muscle in your body aches as you crawl into bed for the night. Supporters of Democrats in Hollywood are basically just like politicians when it comes to honest work. They think they've worked really hard when they finish a fifteen-minute scene in such warm temperatures as eighty degrees. Some people work in atmospheres that reach as high as 150 degrees or more inside of buildings with roaring machines requiring ear protection, but they cannot do anything to mitigate the heat radiating off the hot steel other than taking frequent breaks and drink plenty of water. Those poor, overworked actors must retire to the nearest air-conditioned pub for their afternoon sip of scotch or gin to relieve the tensions of what they believe is real work.

But those folks who live in mansions (politicians and actors) all seem to believe that those who work for a living should surrender all of their earnings in the name of utopian ideals that have never worked. In a practical world, utopian societies will never work, and history has proven they don't work, but that is not the point in communist doctrine. The point is that they want to take everything from us so they can seize absolute "political power."[8] Marx and Engels complained that critics of their insane doctrine said it destroyed personal liberty and freedom. The critics were right. Marx and Engels were wrong.

Meanwhile, I wonder if the Obamas and the Clintons are leaving their entire estates to the federal government. After all, in their own fevered minds, they did nothing to earn their money. Now, some might agree with them on that point.

Chapter Six

LET'S TRY THAT SOVIET TRICK; MAKE THEM CRIMINALS AND TAKE THEIR STUFF

The rationale for Plank number 4 of *The Communist Manifesto* can be summed up in the twelve simple words heading this chapter. In *The Manifesto*, it reads, "Confiscation of the property of all emigrants and rebels."[1] The entire Manifesto is about taking away all of the assets of the working class. Each individual Plank is simply the road map by which that end will be accomplished. If governments cannot legally take one's possessions, then they create crimes, using that as a pretext for "confiscation."

The "administrative state" in America, without a Congressional vote, "issues thousands of regulations and rules" annually,[2] effectively criminalizing Americans, especially the middle class, thus giving the government free reign to strip Americans of their assets if they find them in violation of their oppressive rules. Usually, this is the work of supporters of the Democratic Party, but not to be outdone, a few crafty, power-hungry Republicans seem to view this unconstitutional rule by fiat as nothing more than business as usual. For centuries, monarchs of Europe ruled in this manner. Meanwhile, Americans watch helplessly as their freedoms are being systematically stripped away, and the Constitution is being trampled underfoot. Federal regulation is so complex that Congress, in direct violation of the Constitution, often delegates its powers to a multitude of government agencies.[3] Congress doesn't even know what most of the regulations are, and cannot explain their purpose if they do know the rule.

If a person becomes a criminal, then in many cases, that person is subject to the loss of some, if not all, of his/her property. Sounds reasonable until we examine what our government, especially Democratic wolves, have done to create crime and criminals. The more criminals the government can toss into prison, the more property the government can seize. But let's ignore the Constitution, say the plotters in secret, the people will never know. This cannot be said often enough; Obama, the Clintons, and Bernie Sanders believe we are imbeciles without sense enough to even take out the trash. Even Americans with rudimentary education levels should understand that these people are looking down their long noses at them. They deem themselves our superiors.

Criminalizing America

Since 2001, there have been 38,700 regulations issued by numerous federal agencies without a single vote cast by Congress. "In 2010 alone," there were 3,573 such rules "enacted." "The total number of criminal offenses in the United States Code is actually unknown even to the federal government."[4] That statement from Mark Levin is not only astonishing, it is downright alarming. If Americans think that Big Brother has yet to arrive, they had best wake up. Big Brother is here, and has been watching us for some time. He showed up using stealth, sneaking into our midst while we were not on the alert.

The proliferation of rule by fiat, bypassing Congress and the Constitution, includes hundreds of rules affecting home construction, as well as what one has in the privacy of their own home, such as "light bulbs, cell phones, stereo equipment, and lawn darts," to name only a few. Yes, even lawn darts. Automobile regulations have contributed to soaring price increases for new automobiles and trucks. Unrealistic emission standards have increased the cost of fuels, both gasoline and diesel. Compliance with food standards costs more than the annual earnings of America's farms![5] Why do we need a label on a bottle of water that tells us there are no calories in water? That label is useless, and it needlessly increases the cost of the bottle of water. I could fill hundreds, if not thousands, of pages with examples of waste mandated by the federal government, but if one is not in compliance, then they are subjected to criminal action.

During the administration of Bill Clinton, two laws were passed that have impacted thousands of American lives by making criminals of them. One is the Violent Crime Control and Law Enforcement Act of 1994 (Federal Crime Bill, for short), and the other is the Anti-Terrorism and Effective Death Penalty Act of 1996.

Let's examine the Federal Crime Bill utilizing an online analytical piece by C. Stone Brown. How did the Clinton people convince Congress and its constituents that the bill was necessary? By utilizing mass media to repeatedly display the worst of actual crimes. In other words, through fearmongering, a mainstay of Democratic Party tactics, but Republicans jumped on the bandwagon on this one. The Fourth Amendment prohibits searches of private property without a warrant, and police cannot obtain a warrant without probable cause. The Crime Bill circumvents the Fourth Amendment if an officer thinks "they could have obtained a warrant." The FBI, the ATF, and the DEA, as well as other federal agencies, can knock down your door in the middle of the night and severely humiliate you without cause. If they find no justification for their actions, it doesn't matter.[6] This kind of rigorous approach to fighting "crime" is exactly the kind of tactic employed by Hitler's SS and Gestapo, and it can be implemented by the United States government against anybody who speaks out against government overreach.

The anti-terrorism bill also circumvents the Constitution by allowing all of the above-mentioned agencies to spy on its citizens if they are "suspected" of terrorism. Making one a "suspect" is the part that grants these agencies wide latitude in their operations.[7] You can be sitting in a restaurant and say something like this: "I cannot stand the president. He's kind of a jerk." If the wrong person hears that statement, you may find yourself on the terrorist watch list. You might even find yourself under arrest for threatening the president, and in forfeiture of all of your possessions. This is classic Marxism under Plank 4. Marx used the word "rebel." Our government uses the words "criminal" or "terrorist," unless you are Barack Obama, who refused to refer to real terrorists as terrorists. Meanwhile, powerful figures in the Democratic Party who have allegedly committed criminal acts seem to be immune to investigation by the FBI or other appropriate agencies.

Executive Order 11490

Executive Order 11490, signed into law by Richard Nixon, details the steps the federal government may take if an "emergency" is deemed a threat to the security of the United States. While Nixon was a very intelligent president who did make some significant accomplishments while in office, he resigned under heavy clouds of distrust and ignominy for his misguided efforts to cover up the Watergate burglary. He was also known as a man who craved power, and this Executive Order gave him sweeping powers to commandeer practically any asset in the United States: your money, your home, your business, your automobiles, your retirement funds, your job.[8] Some might argue that a reputable president would never exercise those powers. Read my comments again on Nixon's reputation in the aftermath of Watergate. Could he, or any other person thirsty for power, be trusted NOT to use any little pretext as an emergency? As long as Executive Order 11490 exists, the possibility of some future president utilizing it to seize unwarranted power exists.

This is precisely what I. V. Lenin and Joseph Stalin did in order to implement communism in the Soviet Union. Hundreds of thousands of Russian citizens were deemed "rebels" and shipped off to Siberia, the gulag. Many were never heard from again, and every single asset that they possessed was seized by the state. Records of their existence, birth certificates, diplomas, any type of license issued, were also destroyed so the Soviets could deny that that person ever existed. We in the United States have a Constitution which is supposed to protect us from such tyranny. With the laws discussed in brief in this chapter, the specter of tyranny is hovering over us on a daily basis.

Obama Creates Criminals

Let's turn again to Barack Obama and his signature law, the (un) Affordable Care Act. While the act did not proscribe incarceration, it did have one provision that effectively criminalized innocent people and stole their money, and this impacted far more people than were able to afford the unaffordable insurance. The mandated "fine" for not having some kind of health insurance was illegal. If the Supreme Court had been unbiased and judged the entire bill strictly on the basis of the Constitution, which is what they are supposed to do, they would at least have found this provision unconstitutional. The writers of the bill called the mandate a "fine" because they were loath to use the word "tax." The Supreme Court turned the tables on Americans and called it, and much of the bill, a "tax." That was the only way they could justify their unlawful ruling. Again, those who think the Supreme Court is always right, must ask themselves if the *Dred Scott v. Sanford* or *Plessy v. Ferguson* decisions were just. Both of those decisions were wrong, and the Supreme Court committed a gross error in judgment when they ruled in favor of the Abominable Care Act.

Why did Democrats who controlled Congress in 2010 when the (un) Affordable Care Act was passed think they had the right to levy a "fine" on persons who had no health insurance? Read through Article I of the Constitution. There is no provision whereby Congress can make criminals of law-abiding people. There is also nothing in the Constitution that gives Congress the power to force people to buy something they either cannot afford or do not want. Read Plank 4 of *The Communist Manifesto* and you find the basis for what Congress did. By the way, only Democrats in both houses of Congress and two Independents in the Senate voted for the (un) Affordable Care Act. It is worth noting that some Democrats opposed the taxing monstrosity. In the end, billions of dollars have been confiscated from law-abiding citizens because they are "criminals," since not buying health insurance is now a crime punishable by forfeiture of some of your property.

Loretta Lynch, former Attorney General under Barack Obama, expressed the desire to make it a crime for opposing the pseudoscience of climate change.[9] It seems the FBI, once considered the protector of Americans and their freedoms, has become the enforcement arm of the Democratic Party, similar to Hitler's Gestapo and the KGB in the Soviet Union. As they doggedly pursue any little pretext for which to crucify President Trump, they leave untouched any allegations that certain notable Democrats have committed actual crimes. In other words, the FBI is now a political organization used to suppress conservative ideology and support left-wing dogma. Americans must now live in fear that if they oppose the Democratic Party, they might find themselves under heavy scrutiny from the FBI, and ultimately be tossed into prison for political reasons, one's politics now being a crime.

The Internal Revenue Service

The Internal Revenue Service has become a monstrous bureaucratic agency within the massive framework of government bureaucracy, and they are in possession of excessive and oppressive powers, with the capabilities to destroy any person in America. Why is that agency, which employs well over 100,000 people, so large and powerful? Why is the IRS larger than every single American corporation? Why does it take so many people to collect our tax dollars? And why do they often overstep their authority, confiscating the financial assets of thousands of persons?

The simple answer to these questions is because they can hire all the people, they deem necessary and use them as they see fit. The complex answer is just as complex as the tax codes. Nonetheless, in the history of the IRS, they have needlessly and ruthlessly destroyed the financial security of thousands of people for two reasons; the first is because they are usually not flexible enough to work with individuals who, for varied reasons, are already in financial trouble; second, it is much easier as well as more desirable to simply take all of your possessions and hand them to the government. To be fair, many of their victims are persons who have made deliberate efforts to avoid paying income taxes, as did George Parr, the Duke of Duval County, Texas.[10] But the IRS was granted the power to collect the illegal "fine" imposed by the (un)Affordable Care Act. They, like the Supreme Court, also will never admit they have made mistakes, and try to rectify them by restoring assets to those they have wronged. The IRS is the quintessential "Big Brother" agency, an illegal confiscatory arm of the government.

Hollywood Creates Terrorists

We've already noted that Barack Obama would never refer to terrorists as such, nor would he use the phrase "radical Islam." In 2014, the film industry released the first of the television series *TURN: Washington's Spies*, and it ran for four seasons. Being unable to get enough of history, I thought I'd enjoy the series, but the first time I heard an actor playing the part of a British officer refer to the Americans as "terrorists," I changed the channel and never went back. Portraying the British army referring to the revolutionaries as "terrorists" is a gross and deliberate historical inaccuracy.

The British may have referred to the rebellious colonists as "rebels" or even "traitors," but never as terrorists.

Hollywood's use of the term is most undoubtedly an attempt to cast aspersions on the makers of the American Revolution, fully supporting Democratic Party opposition to every ideology espoused by the revolutionaries, and redirecting the entire episode in world history as one in support of slavery. The Revolution was not about supporting slavery, neither was the writing of the Constitution.

Hollywood was also trying to redefine the word "terrorist." The colonists were using military units to fight against other military units, not running pell-mell into a crowded room of innocents and triggering a bomb in order to slaughter women and children. But Hollywood had to lend credence to the ideas of their darling in the White House. Real terrorists are not really terrorists, in Obama's fevered mind, but people who do not employ terrorism as a tactical weapon are really terrorists. Such ludicrous logic is pure Hollywood propaganda in support of the left-wing statists in the Democratic Party.

Emigration

As seen in Plank 4, Marx also believed that if one left his/her country behind, that person should also leave behind all of their possessions. Seizing the possessions of an emigrant is a common practice in all totalitarian regimes, largely because one must "escape" from those places under cover of night, so it is often difficult to bring much with you other than the clothes on your back. We see this in Middle Eastern states today, but all who fled the Soviet Union and any of its satellite states were unable to keep anything other than what they could carry.

When the Democratic Party finally creates a totalitarian state of the United States, we will be treated the same. However, we'll have a singular problem that other refugees in the entire history of the world were not faced with; we'll have nowhere to go for sanctuary, no means of escaping tyranny. There will be no port in the storm as the entire world will have succumbed to tyranny. And, quite possibly, the 1 billion acres the government has confiscated will become our gulags. Maybe they will put us behind fences on this land and take all of our possessions.

Chapter Seven

WE NEED TO MAKE IT LOOK LIKE WE'RE NOT STEALING

The *Communist Manifesto*, Plank 5, calls for the establishment of a national bank. It reads, "Centralization of credit in the hands of the state, by means of a national bank with state capital and an exclusive monopoly."[1] An "exclusive monopoly!" Does anybody see anything wrong with that notion!? I do! The United States government has expended a fortune prosecuting monopoly, and breaking them up, yet the Democratic Party justifies holding a government "monopoly" in the banking business. Why? Because it's easier to control if all power is concentrated in a central government, something the founders were also loath to allow.

Long before Marx and Engels penned this smoke screen for the concentration of economic power, Alexander Hamilton had proposed a national bank, and set about convincing the Washington administration it was a grand idea. Hamilton, to be honest, was not trying to steal anything. His main agenda was to create a solvent United States government, with enough operating funds to carry on its business. Nonetheless, he opened the proverbial Pandora's Box.

The anti-Federalists, led by Thomas Jefferson, wholeheartedly opposed a national bank. They argued that the Constitution does not grant explicit powers to Congress to establish a national bank, nor does it grant that power to any other branch of the federal government. Their argument was correct. James Madison, who is often considered the father of the Constitution, also disagreed with Hamilton's bank, citing the 9th and 10th Amendments. These two amendments were designed to leave certain rights not explicitly granted to the central government in the hands of "the people" and "the states" respectively. Madison argued that the creation of a central bank was unconstitutional because these two amendments left that power to the control of individual business persons or individual states.[2] Try to find any mention of a central bank in the Constitution; the language does not exist, therefore it is not an explicit power granted to Congress.

But Alexander Hamilton, a staunch Federalist, was a very persistent man, and he hit upon language that does exist in the Constitution. It is often referred to as the elastic clause, and can be found in the last paragraph of Section 8 of Article I. Section 8 mostly spells out the explicit powers of Congress, but the final paragraph, Hamilton said, gave Congress "implied" powers. It says, "To make all Laws which shall be necessary and proper for carrying into Execution the foregoing powers…" The word "proper" was problematic in the debate on the bank. Anti-federalists, to support their stance, said the bank wasn't proper. Federalists said it was. In the end, the Federalists prevailed and a national bank became an institution of the new republic.[3]

The landmark Supreme Court case, *McCulloch v. Maryland* (1819), was an early challenge to the existence of the Bank of the United States. At that point in time, the original charter had expired, but it had been renewed following the usual arguments that it should never have existed in the first place. The case that eventually reached the Supreme Court involved a tax that the state of Maryland had imposed on the federal bank, but James McCulloch, a clerk for the bank's branch in Baltimore, was refusing to pay the tax. Essentially, the federal government filed the case to challenge the Maryland tax with McCulloch as plaintiff, opposing the state of Maryland as the defendant. The high court ruled in favor of the federal government, stating that the bank was "a legitimate end," meaning it was "proper" in order for Congress to carry out its duties, and that states could not interfere with the operation of the national bank by taxing it.[4] I have already established the fact that the Supreme Court is not infallible.

Like so many issues in American History, the existence of a national bank continued to be criticized. The charter for the Second Bank of the United States was set to expire in 1836, but both houses of Congress passed a bill in 1832, an election year, to ensure the bank would live beyond its expiration date, and the bill went to the desk of the angriest president in the nation's history, the founder of the Democratic Party, Andrew Jackson. In the 1830s, the Democratic Party, while staunchly supporting slavery, was opposed to the growth of big government. Many of Jackson's ideologies were aligned with the South, and to a great extent, the West. Western agriculturalists had been hurt several times by the bank's credit policies. Jackson vetoed the bill, and the national bank died until 1913, during the Progressive Era.[5]

Andrew Jackson's veto did nothing to help western farmers who owed large debts to numerous banks. In fact, it had mostly adverse effects, and the debate did not die with Andrew Jackson. Karl Marx revived the issue in Plank 5 of *The Manifesto*, and American Progressives, under Woodrow Wilson, breathed new life into a government institution that, in fact, was never intended to exist.

The Federal Reserve Act of 1913 created a new national bank with broad and sweeping powers to control the money supply of the United States as well as the economic health of the nation. It was born out of Progressive ideology which was largely rooted in Plank 5 of Marxist doctrine. Woodrow Wilson had no qualms about such sweeping socialist/communist "reform." After all, he had no issues with a graduated income tax. Nor did he seem to have any issue with exercising absolute power over the nation. The Federal Reserve Act created regional banks throughout the United States, and forced all banks with a national charter to transfer six percent of their capital assets to the new national bank. Also, those same banks had to surrender some of their reserve operating funds. The new law created a Federal Reserve Board, often called the "Fed," and the Fed sets the prime lending rates, interest rates that member banks have to pay when they borrow from the Fed.[6] Had Karl Marx been alive, he would have characterized Woodrow Wilson, a Democrat, as a good communist.

For more than 100 years, this new bank has exercised almost totalitarian power over America's economy. Meanwhile, Democrats, since the Progressive Era, have pointed the finger continuously at major United

States corporations, blaming them for every economic disaster that has befallen the nation. However, the Great Depression can be laid firmly at the feet of the Federal Reserve System and its policies aimed at controlling every aspect of the economy, but especially the volume of money that was in circulation at the time. They had been lending money with reckless abandon. When the Depression struck, they imposed more restrictive loan policies, but the cattle had already got out of the pasture; it was too late to close the gate.

In the final analysis, the Fed has far more power over our economic welfare than the framers of the Constitution would have imagined possible. It didn't stop in 1913. Subsequent laws have granted them even more powers. During the Great Depression, the New Deal programs of Franklin Roosevelt included the Federal Deposit Insurance Corporation, which supposedly insures one's deposits against loss. The FDIC is a smoke screen, as is much of the surviving New Deal programs. If we experience another economic collapse similar to that of 1929, bank deposits would dry up and the government would have absolutely no way to make good with "insurance." The politicians with the fattest thumbs on the nation's economy will be the only wealthy people left, and the rest of us will become their serfs. Margolis and Noonan cite an excellent example of how the FDIC will ignore the average bank depositor in favor of the powerful.[7]

William Jefferson Clinton, a good Democratic Socialist, and an adherent to communist ideologies, greatly encouraged "risky" mortgage practices including loans to people with bad credit history. The Federal Housing Administration, acceding to pressure from the White House, did just that, leading to the infamous subprime housing crash of 2007-2008. In reality, people who could not afford a huge mortgage were told they could.[8] The government was going to make good on that deal as well. Who held the paper on the subprime mortgages? Lending institutions, banks that borrowed from the Fed. When those who could not pay their mortgages were foreclosed on, who ultimately bore the brunt of the losses? Not the Fed, or even the banks, but the taxpayers of America who shelled out billions of dollars in the form of bailouts.

The subprime disaster culminated in tremendous losses for Americans in every station of life, but they hit the middle class the hardest. Home values plunged, even for those who could afford to pay their mortgages.

Millions of middle class Americans witnessed the value of their retirement funds decrease by as much as 50 percent. The government eventually paid billions in "bailout" money to the major banks, and other corporations to keep them solvent, but the average working-class American derived little benefit, if any, from those "bailouts." The people who made out like bandits, which is generally considered to be less than ten human beings on this planet, are still out there because there were no laws forbidding their greedy actions, and they, along with their close cronies in the government at the time, are enjoying the hundreds of billions of dollars they stole from middle class Americans.

Remember, Karl Marx wanted the middle class, especially the upper-middle class, the bourgeoisie, the entrepreneur, to disappear. Our homes, in the housing market collapse of 2008, came very close to becoming federal property which would have been a huge step toward destroying the middle class. The Democratic Party, when they have power over the federal banking system as they did under Bill Clinton, would have reveled if they could have seized millions of homes. At least under the leadership of Andrew Jackson, the Democratic Party eschewed a national bank. However, under Woodrow Wilson, the Democrats have fallen in line with Marxist doctrine, and have supported the bank ever since, and Barack Obama used it as a tool to pilfer from the middle class by handing billions of tax dollars to banks and various other corporations. I doubt his intentions were to keep them afloat, but rather to force them to become beholden to the government in perpetuity so that the government could, in reality, run them; in other words, implement fascist statism.

Chapter Eight

BIG BROTHER LISTENS TO YOU

Plank 6 of *The Communist Manifesto* is one of the most disturbing of all of them, if one carefully ponders its implications. Its emphasis is on thought control by monitoring what one says in almost any public forum, such as television and radio, and it is a tactic employed by every single communist regime in history. Under Lenin and Stalin, "all negative information about the country was suppressed." Both of these tyrants created government organizations that not only tightly controlled expression of thought, but punished severely those who ventured beyond the guidelines.[1] The United States federal government already has organizations and punishments that are similar in nature. According to Mark Levin, the old Greek philosopher, Plato, as well as Thomas More, and Thomas Hobbes, in their descriptions of utopian societies, included the notion that a police state implemented by a totalitarian government was necessary to ensure compliance.[2] We are closer to a police state than many of us are willing to admit.

Plank 6 calls for control of all the transportation and communication systems within a communist state. The wording is as follows: "Centralization of the means of communication and transport in the hands of the state."[3] It is very important to note the use of the word "centralization." It was the first word of Plank 5 as well. When that word is used, it often implies absolute power to control one or more aspects of society. In all communist states, the governments had absolute power over all political, economic, and social aspects of life. In Planks 5 and 6, the state controls all banks and the money supply, as well as communication and transportation systems.

Communication

The United States largely controls all means of communication through the Federal Communications Commission, an organization founded in 1934 under probably the most revered socialist president in our history, Franklin Delano Roosevelt. The FCC regulates everything people can say on the radio, including privately operated ham radios, television, and what we say over the telephone, including cellular phones.[4] With the passage of time, the FCC has grown increasingly more powerful, utilizing those powers often to suppress conservative ideologies while supporting liberal bias. As of the day of this writing, the vast majority of so-called "news" spews nothing but venomous slander at the Republican Party, while Democrats are held in high esteem. Indeed, it seemed that for eight long years, Barack Obama walked on water. He could do no wrong in the adoring eyes of the biased news media, even while imposing exorbitant taxes on the middle class, mollycoddling Islamic terrorists while tacitly expressing disdain for Christianity and Judaism, and circumventing constitutional authority by issuing hundreds, if not thousands, of executive orders.

Meanwhile, the FCC, as well as other organizations, very efficiently shut down any criticism of Obama. One example of suppression of opposition to the rise of statism in America was the cancellation of Tim Allen's sitcom, *Last Man Standing*. Tim Allen's character on the series, Mike Baxter, portrays an American conservative, a hardworking individual who has made his mark in the business world. Baxter does not like Obama, Hillary or Bill Clinton, John Kerry, Al Gore, or any of the rest of the politicians bent on destroying the Constitution and replacing it with a statist dictatorship. While the FCC may not have been the culprit in the cancellation of the television series, they do allow sitcoms and comedians that drone on incessantly about the "horrors" of Christianity and capitalism to continue *ad nauseum*, while those who oppose such dangerous ideologies are being closely monitored as if the conservatives are the ones promoting the demise of democracy in America.

Other examples of how much power the FCC has can be found in the Patriot Act. The federal government can monitor all emails, telephone calls, and other forms of electronic communication. I am not so paranoid that I believe them to be listening to everybody because that task would be herculean. But I am convinced that if you speak out against Democrats, and somebody hears you who disagrees with your assertions, you stand a strong chance of becoming one of their targets. As a matter of fact, if this gets published, they will probably put me on their watch list. I don't much care because I believe the 1st Amendment applies to all, not just to Democrats who want to destroy the Constitution, which ironically includes their 1st Amendment rights. Actually, Democrats believe the 1st Amendment applies only to them, and only when it suits their subversive purposes.

Comedians have become the worst perpetrators of professing their political beliefs with wanton abandon. They can say whatever they wish, true or false, as long as it's anti-Republican. They can promote the idea of killing Donald Trump, as in the case of Kathy Griffin, who held up the bloodied, severed effigy of Trump's head. She did lose her job, but the communist pundits in the entertainment industry poured out of the woodwork in her support. One argument posed by Miss Griffin's supporters was that she was treated differently than a conservative would have been had they done the same thing with the head of Barack Obama. That argument is accurate; had she been a conservative who displayed an effigy of Obama's severed head, she would not only have lost her job, but she would have been arrested, tried, convicted, and sent to prison for making a death threat against the president.

In the final analysis, the 1st Amendment does not protect one from proposing or promoting murder, which is exactly what Griffin was doing. Was she arrested? Of course not. Communism promotes the notion of the violent overthrow of the government, therefore she was simply supporting that extremist left-wing ideology, and the Democrats/Socialists/ Communists/ Statists love her for her passionate display of hatred. FCC regulations seem to apply only to those who support Republican, or conservative, ideals. Democrats are allowed to use the airwaves to foment a rebellion, in absolute disregard for the personal liberties of all Americans.

There are somewhere between 1.5 and 2 million persons globally who are operators of ham radios, over 800,000 of which are in the United States and are subject to FCC regulations.[5] The vast majority of those who own and operate ham radio equipment are hobbyists who like to reach around the world to see who they can contact and what is going on in other parts of the world. They are not furthering an overthrow of the United States government, as the Hollywood 10 did in many of their films. However, anything they say on the air is closely monitored, unlike the Hollywood 10, who were allowed, for a time, to insert communist doctrine into their films. The screenwriters who made up the Hollywood 10, and many of the actors and actresses and others who had anything to do with the film industry were acolytes of Joseph Stalin, bent on destroying the United States of America.[6] Ignoring the fact that Joe Stalin was a mass murderer, and much to the delight of the Hollywood 10, Franklin Roosevelt referred to Stalin as "Uncle Joe," a nice tribute from one socialist to another.[7]

When the dust had cleared and time had passed, the Hollywood 10, who hated free press if it was used to oppose them, has been raised to adulatory status by today's filmmakers. Not so the ham radio operator. That person is always suspected of harboring harmful ideas about destroying the United States, thus they are subjected to rules and regulations that can be their downfall, depending upon how their broadcast comments are interpreted. Prohibitive speech is spelled out somewhat vaguely in Part 97, Section 97.113 of the regulations on ham radio operation. It prohibits "deceptive messages," but does not clearly define them. "Obscene or indecent language" also goes undefined, therefore leaving interpretation up to the court system, a system that can exercise wide latitude in its interpretations.[8] A person who might mention his/ her political or religious beliefs over the airwaves might be construed as having broadcast a "deceptive message." It might even be considered indecent or offensive, but Hollywood scriptwriters can use any language in their scenes and their comedian's monologues, as well as promote an ideology they deem better than democracy. Utilizing these kinds of regulations, the socialists/ communists can exercise control over the right-wing's rights to freedom of speech.

Transportation

A mountain of regulation exists in the transportation industry, the least of which is the requirements to register your automobile and to carry a driver's license, which fits perfectly with Plank 6 of *The Manifesto*; "centralization of the means of . . . transport in the hands of the state." One argument favoring that type of regulation is that it makes our highways safer for motorists, including truck drivers, and safer for highway patrolmen in every state. In fact, it does not. A 20-year-old motorist in the hill country of Texas recently killed 13 elderly persons in a church van. He was licensed. His vehicle was duly registered. Neither fact prevented the tragedy. Allegedly he had been texting on an extremely winding and hilly highway for some time before the collision. There may be other issues, but I'll not discuss them here because there are pending actions between that driver, the state of Texas, and the families of the persons who perished in the accident. The obvious lesson is that the state's collection of registration and licensing fees did not make the highway safe for the people who died in the crash.

Admittedly, one should have to pass an exam and illustrate some proficiency in the operation of a motor vehicle in order to be issued a driver's license. But the real reasons a license is required are twofold: first, the state can collect yet another fee, a tax; secondly, the state can ascertain your identity and utilize it for various purposes, including your capture in the event you have committed a crime. But they can also use that information to collect information on your "subversive" activities, especially if you disagree with liberal politicians. Registering one's auto also accomplishes both of the above. Safety is not a tantamount concern. We are slaughtering somewhere around 40,000 persons annually on the nation's highways. The mandated documentation of vehicles and drivers obviously does nothing to prevent those deaths, but they go a long way toward government intrusion into our personal liberty.

Not to be outdistanced by the individual states, the federal government has its own set of regulations under the auspices of the Department of Transportation, the Federal Aviation Administration, and others. These bureaucratic departments impose mountains of burdensome requirements on both commercial and private carriers of freight and passengers, land and air, giving the government the power to closely monitor our movements within and beyond the borders of the nation.

Let's briefly explore the impact on the private owner of his/her own commercial truck. For starters, this person is disliked by the socialists

(Democratic Party) because they usually fit within the middle class. Some might even be upper-middle class. As we have seen, according to Marxist principles, these are the people who must disappear so they can pose no challenges to a statist regime. Oppressive regulation is only the first step toward achieving the desired outcome; make the lives of owner/operators miserable by imposing heavy taxes on the operation of their rigs, and incessantly raising the costs of licenses and truck registrations in order to make the cost of operation prohibitive. In due time the federal government can seize absolute power over the trucking industry, including government ownership of the same, because individuals will no longer be able to afford their own operations.

Major airlines that carry passengers or freight, or both, are subjected to identical prohibitive restraints. And the avalanche grows stronger and more burdensome with the passage of each new power given to the FAA (Federal Aviation Administration). Those of us who are my age have already witnessed the demise of a number of airlines, including Braniff. Somehow others manage to survive the federal government's attacks on their operations, but they do so by sacrificing such things as comfort. New planes are crowded. The seats are too close together. By using smaller seating, they can increase the number of fares on a flight in order to offset the impact of exorbitant taxes and other charges imposed by the FAA.

But the goal of Democrats is complete control of all airlines, and once they have achieved that goal, we will see them operated inefficiently on a grand scale. Historically, we know that Amtrak, which is government-controlled, operates at a tremendous loss annually. Of course, it makes sense to let the government, which cannot operate a lemonade stand in the black, take over the airline industry. After all, they are already only one step away from owning all of the railroads, not just Amtrak.

The USSR took over all means of transportation under Lenin and Stalin. Russia operated them disastrously throughout the existence of the Soviet Union, but had to begin releasing them to private individuals in the 1980s, the last decade of the existence of the USSR, in order to salvage what remained of dilapidated rail and air systems. But they had been simply following Marxism to the letter. The Democratic Party wants to do the same in the United States even though history has proven that Marxism was a failure. Historically, we have our Amtrak experience. No private sector company of any nature would still be in business after only a couple of years of operating with tremendous losses. Our government simply forces us to burn up tax dollars to subsidize a grossly mismanaged and wasteful system.

The United States Postal Service does no better than Amtrak, operating year after year in the red. There are a number of reasons neither of the institutions will ever be profitable, and I will discuss some of them in Chapter 10 when we explore Plank 8. For now, suffice it to say that the government does not care if they turn a profit. Why, then, do leftists want the government to completely control all businesses, including communications and transportation? It's not about efficiency because the federal government has proved it cannot operate a business with any degree of efficiency; it's about absolute power. It's about totalitarianism, complete control in the hands of the state. With the centralization of banking (Plank 5) and of transportation and communication (Plank 6), the government can reduce our economic freedom and suppress our 1st Amendment rights to freedom of speech and of lawful assembly.

Chapter Nine

THE GOVERNMENT BUILT IT; GIVE IT BACK

One of the most ridiculous planks of Marxism, and one heavily supported by Democrats, is Plank number 7. It's the one that calls for state ownership of the means of production, although Democrats thinly disguise their agenda as equalization of the wealth of the state. Here is the entire text of Plank 7: "Extension of factories and instruments of production owned by the state; the bringing into cultivation of wastelands, and the improvement of the soil generally in accordance with a common plan."[1] As evidenced by massive government waste and inefficiency, the history of the Soviet Union notwithstanding, this is pure rubbish.

When Stalin implemented his Five-Year Plan in the late 1920s and early 1930s, he stripped ownership of land from approximately 25 million farmers, placing all of the lands under the control of the state. Productivity immediately plunged because persons who were assigned the task of operating the farms had no incentive to do their best. A good worker got no more or no less than a lousy one, therefore workers did only enough to satisfy those in charge of them. Joseph Stalin then stood idly aside as tragedy struck the very people he purported to be the champions of, the "proletariat" of workers, starved to death. Estimates of the death toll range from 3 million to more than 14 million,[2] but most sources place it around 7 million deaths.[3] America's farmers assisted in staving off further starvation by shipping billions of tons of grain and other food crops to the USSR annually. Promoting the notion of state-owned, collectivized farms, is where the Democratic Party agenda takes on a most sinister undertone.

DDT and Fearmongering

The Democratic Party in the United States thinks they can do the same thing with the farms that Joseph Stalin did, but with much better results; or is that what they really think? In the 1970s, Democrats, with the complicity of many Republicans, successfully campaigned to outlaw the safest and most effective pesticide in history, DDT (di-chloro-diphenyl-trichloroethane), falsely convinced, as we now know, that the birds of the world were going to be wiped out by its use. Rachel Carson, using false science, penned Silent Spring, fully intending to outlaw the use of DDT. Was she really trying to save birds? Evidence exists that the bird population had continually increased from the time DDT went into use after World War II until her slanted tale of doom was published in 1962.

But let's shift gears a moment and talk about that other species of bipods that walk upright on the earth; human beings. As stated, DDT was an effective pesticide, therefore decreasing crop losses attributable to insects, and in turn, increasing food crop yields, crops that literally helped to feed the world, including the millions suffering in the Soviet Union. It was also very effective at destroying mosquitoes by the millions, making life more pleasant for those residing in temperate zones in sub-Saharan Africa and Central America. The incidence of malaria and other tropical diseases decreased dramatically with the use of DDT, sparing the lives of millions of African and Latin American children.

In spite of growing evidence that DDT was safe, even for birds, the fearmongers prevailed and DDT was banned. In turn, the United States put pressure on the sub-Saharan African states to quit using it or be faced with the loss of aid. All too late, the truth now speaks for itself. DDT is so safe that one man, Professor Kenneth Mellanby, ate some at every lecture he delivered during the course of 40 years.[4] Meanwhile, farmers had to scramble to find a new pesticide while they watched their crops being destroyed by insects. The most tragic end of the tale is that something close to 750,000 children in sub-Saharan African states have died from malaria, which reared its ugly head again as the mosquito population spiraled upward.[5] Was DDT banned in order to protect birds, or was it a measure to control the world's population?

Organic Crops

Another push by left-wing fear-mongers in the Democratic Party today is to completely eliminate all fertilizers, pesticides, and other chemical methods that enable America's farmers to be the best in the world at the cultivation of food crops. Most Americans don't realize that much of what our farmers grow is exported. There aren't enough of us to eat all of it, so it has to go someplace. We have been the breadbasket of the world since the end of the 19th century. If we are forced to completely shift to organic crop production, our farm output will be a mere 15% of where it currently stands. Fifteen percent! And organic foods, without the aid of fertilizers to replenish nutrients in the soil, will be lacking in basic nutrition.

Starvation will ensue on a horrific scale never before witnessed in the entire history of the world. What Stalin did to his own people will pale by comparison. I am talking about the very real possibility that several billion people could starve to death. But that may not even be the worst of it. Millions more will die because they will become sources of food for those in dire need. All of this will happen in the course of three to five years, much like it did on a smaller scale in the Soviet Union. Some of us in the United States might read this and think it cannot possibly happen to us. Yes, it can. The U. S. most assuredly will not go unfazed by such a drastic reduction in food crops.

Do Democrats honestly believe they can implement collectivized farming and organic farming and produce positive results? Or is this another policy aimed at population control? The answer depends on what you think they want. If you think their interest is in a healthier environment, then you need to start at the beginning of the chapter and read it again. If you think it's all a ruse to implement population control, then you are catching on. If they want total control, or totalitarianism, then they can best achieve that by reducing the population of the world by several billion people, maybe more, and most especially eliminate that hated middle class. In this manner, they can minimize any challenges to their authority. Maximilien Robespierre, who implemented the "Reign of Terror" during the French Revolution, was eliminating his enemies by sending them to the guillotine. Democrats are not being so direct, but the end result will be even more horrible. None of them will admit to such a sinister objective, but pay close attention to their not-so-subtle subtleties at times. Even Bill Nye, the Science Guy, said a lot of people need to die to save the planet.[6] Is it really to save the planet? No. Just study the history of communism to arrive at the true answer.

Collectivized Farming

Collectivized farming failed in the Soviet Union. It failed in Cuba. It failed in Venezuela. It failed in Eastern Europe during the Cold War. It will fail anywhere it is implemented. Crop failures in the USSR were so precipitous that the theft of food became a prevailing way of life until Stalin implemented the death penalty for such a crime.[7] If Democrats have their way, and force it upon us here, it will have global implications that will outstrip anything we have seen in all the horror films in the history of film combined.

The process is already being gradually, and ever so subtly, implemented. The U. S. Department of Agriculture has tremendous power over our nation's farmers. While they are not owners of the farms, they do exercise a great deal of control over them. The Environmental Protection Agency can be, and often is, a tool to control farming, especially when it relates to what chemicals farmers have available to them. As mentioned in Chapter 2, the seizure of 1 billion acres of land by the federal government eliminates any possibility of any of that land being used productively to help feed the world's growing population. Of course, not all of it is arable land, such as the ANWR, but much of it could prove to be productive.

Sometime in the future, if your neighbor asks you to dinner, you may want to make sure that you are not going to be the main course.

State-Owned Factories

Joseph Stalin's Five-Year Plan also included state ownership of every kind of production facility one can name, and it's one of a few basic concepts that differentiate communism from fascism. Just as farm production declined, so did factory output decline in the Soviet Union, after an ever-so brief upturn in production. What followed was a disaster. Living standards fell and "real earnings" dropped to about 10% of what they had been prior to the Five-Year Plan.[8] This is what does happen when working-class people are stripped of all incentives to improve job performance, and Soviet factories suffered heavily from disillusioned workers who were deceived into thinking that communism was going to bring unprecedented improvements into their lives. After all, 300 years of tyrannical Romanov Czars had never offered them anything other than eternal peasant status. Lenin, Stalin, and all the communist leaders were no different than the Romanovs;[9] in many ways, they were worse.

The Democratic Party believes the government can run industry best, but what they really want is the destruction of America's industry, especially the oil industry. Destroying the oil industry will not only wreck the American economy, but also wreck the economy of the entire world. Their pretext for destroying oil companies is to protect the environment, but I'll have more on that in a later chapter. For now, suffice it to say that the end of the oil industry will mean millions of jobs lost. Oil companies alone employ hundreds of thousands of people. Additionally, service industries such as drilling operations and contract maintenance workers that rely heavily on the oil industry employ many more people than the oil companies.

Collectively, the United States would see the direct loss of close to 5 million jobs without oil. A domino effect will add anywhere from another 50 million to 75 million lost jobs. School teachers in many regions would face unemployment as schools would no longer be able to operate. City governments would collapse, the transportation industry would grind to a halt, and tourism would cease to exist. Farms, without adequate fuel for tractors and other machinery, would be destroyed. The impact of that event, starvation on an unprecedented scale, has already been discussed.

Other industries that would face destruction would definitely include the automobile industry, followed by such industries as paint, steel, glass, rubber, plastics, and all the businesses that support automobile repairs and parts. It will be an economic disaster that would make the Great Depression seem like a stubbed toe.

Government Motors Corporation

Barack Obama made a subtle, or was it not so subtle, attempt to take over the auto industry with disastrous results for General Motors Corporation. Of the Big Three, only Ford, much to the chagrin of Obama, refused to take any of the bailout funds in 2008. Chrysler accepted bailout money, but has paid it back, thus freeing them from being beholden to big government.

General Motors, however, as of this writing, has not repaid the taxpayers of America, largely due to being coerced by the government to build an automobile on which it has done nothing but lose money. The government pressured GM to build an electric car, and we now know that they built the Volt, an economic disaster. First of all, no family of four or five can fit in a Volt. Secondly, it's difficult to find stations in order to recharge the electric batteries that drive the machine. They are not on every street corner. In fact, the only ones I've ever seen were tucked in behind a mall or on the edge of hotel parking lots, not easily seen or accessed from any major highway.

But the worst thing for GM and its stockholders is that they cannot sell the Volt at a profit because the cost of production is extremely high, and the vast majority of Americans are not going to pay $70,000 for a car that uncomfortably seats about 1 and a half persons. In an effort to unload the unattractive cars, GM began to sell them at a loss. They are still selling them at a tremendous loss, some estimates being as high as $50,000 per unit in the red.[10] That doesn't seem to be a problem for Democrats. After all, they don't seem to mind watching Amtrak and the U. S. Postal Service consume billions of tax payer's dollars annually. If we just let the taxpayers cough up the difference, we can do this forever, think Democrats. No, we cannot. Any private enterprise, corporation or otherwise, that is operating at a loss year after year will eventually have to close its doors or head for bankruptcy court, or both. Margaret Thatcher said it best when she proclaimed, "The trouble with socialism is that you eventually run out of other people's money."[11]

Distribution of Wealth

One of Marx's greatest mistakes is in imagining that state control of production will result in equal distribution of wealth. The USSR proved that it not only does not, it will not. China, Cuba, North Korea, and other communist states have reinforced the failure of the socialist experiment.

The publicly traded corporations of the free world have done a far better job of distributing wealth than any other economic system in history.[12] I am certain that when the left-wingers read that sentence, they will scream, Foul! Foul! Foul! How can that possibly work? The leftist leadership wants the average voter to believe that all corporations are bad because they are owned by powerful family moguls. In the early history of the rise of corporations, that would have been true, but today's modern communists want us to believe it remains the truth.

The key word to focus on is "publicly." Today, anybody who has 10, 20, or 50 dollars they wish to invest can do so by purchasing a share of common stock of any publicly-traded company. If they have more money to invest, they might buy two shares, or 50, or even 1000. This makes them an owner in the enterprise, thus major corporations with millions of shares of outstanding stock have thousands of owners, not one, single, powerful owner. But being a stockholder is only part of the beauty of owning a corporation. As an owner, the person earns dividends on each share of stock depending on the performance of the company. When the company makes money, the owner of each share of stock is paid a dividend. Long-term investors seek out solvent companies in which to invest their hard-earned money. But when a company is losing money, and its stockholders suffer, they will revolt against its board of directors by tossing them out of the board room. If that doesn't turn performance around, then stockholders will divest the stock, and go in search of greener pastures.

Democrats also keep telling us that women don't make what men make, but they are comparing the wages of a female college student waiting tables in a restaurant with that of a male who is a corporate executive. They don't tell us that the Civil Rights Act of 1964 requires the same pay for the same task, but that it applies only to hourly positions. Therefore, if a female and a male are hired on the same day for the job of an operator in a petrochemical plant, both, by law, are going to get the same hourly rate. But corporations are also fair at jobs that pay much more, such as engineers. All engineers where I used to work, male or female, began their career with the same pay. But fast-food workers, who are less skilled, are not going to earn what an engineer earns, no matter their gender. A female high school teacher will earn the same pay as a male high school teacher in the same school, but a female high school teacher will never earn the same pay as any CPA, male or female. Democrats are comparing apples to oranges when they raise this issue.

Returning to the stock owner argument, there are millions of people who own corporations, a fact the Democratic Party will never publicly admit, nor do they want their supporters to know. They want their supporters to believe all that money is ending up in the hands of a few. The only place that is true is in Hollywood, where we find staunch supporters of the Democratic Socialists who pay actresses less than they pay actors. Why will Democrats and the left-wing press never acknowledge that publicly traded corporations benefit millions of people? The answer lies in their quest for power. If they do admit it, then people will find they have at least one less reason to vote for more communism. The mule and the carrot trick will begin losing its luster.

Equal distribution of wealth is but a pipe dream, and the ideologues should know that from the history of communism. At any given moment in time, there is a finite volume of wealth in the entire world, be it in cash, or other assets such as homes, cars, buildings, land, desks and chairs, household furniture, dishes, and so on. As of 2017, if that wealth were to be equally distributed among 7 billion people throughout the world, each person would receive less than $10,000 in assets. Let's suppose your $10,000 is an acre of land on a rocky hillside. What are you going to do with it? It will not sustain crops or livestock, and you will not want your home on a slanting hill. All that aside, you don't have anything with which to construct a home, and you cannot even sell your land because nobody can buy it. In other words, the acre of land became worthless at the very moment equal distribution of wealth occurred. Suppose your asset is a used car. What are you going to do with it? You can't sell it for the same reason the other person cannot sell their acre of land. You can't put gasoline in it and drive it because you will have no money for fuel, in the event fuel is even available. If you were given $10,000 in cash, the cash is immediately worthless; it's just green paper with a face on it.

It should be very evident to all that under the weight of forced equalization of wealth, the global economy will grind to a smashing halt. Everybody will become poor and starve to death; except, of course, let's not forget the wealthy elite, which will include elite Democrats, who will ensure that they get to keep the lion's share of the wealth of the world anyway, thus continuing the saga of unequal wealth. By the way, there will be no more movies, and those Hollywood ideologues who are pushing this economic rubbish will suffer with the rest of us. They just think the party elite will ensure they remain millionaires, an impossibility because nobody will be able to afford a movie and the theaters will be closed.

There will be no National Football League, so we won't have to watch the assault on America when players refuse to stand for the national anthem. There will be no NBA, no American or National League baseball teams, and no television to watch them on anyway.

If anybody thinks that "equal distribution" is what Democrats truly want, they are allowing themselves to be deceived. The socialists/communists want all the wealth for the party elite, and the rest of us will be left to chase after the elusive carrot, but even the carrot will no longer exist. Sound familiar? It's precisely what the Soviet Union was like for about 70 years, and what Cuba has been like since 1959. It has been the same story in every single communist state since Marx and Engels penned their blueprint for the destruction of order in the world. A vote for a Democrat pledging equal distribution of wealth is a vote for communism and the demise of America.

The rest of the world will laugh at us until they realize that they were doing much better when America was economically strong. We are always the first on the scene when typhoons and floods and earthquakes wreak havoc on third world countries, providing billions in food, clothing, medicine, and shelter. When our Democracy is destroyed, and our farms and factories have failed, they will no longer see any kind of aid whatsoever from America. We'll be just like them and the laughter will fade as sober reality takes over.

Chapter Ten

LET'S DRESS THEM ALIKE AND MARCH THEM TO WORK IN STEP

Karl Marx and Friedrich Engels' eighth plank envisioned large happy armies of worker bees marching off to the factory or the farm each morning, whistling gaily as they trudged along or visiting with the man next to them, discussing the children or the next communist approved holiday festivities; but never politics. Plank 8 says, "Equal liability of all to labor. Establishment of industrial armies, especially for agriculture."[1] The two communists overlooked all possibility that the "armies" might become disenchanted with being relegated once again to serfdom, with no reward for outstanding performance, or with being paid no better than the ousted industrialists had paid them.[2] In fact, many did much worse than they were doing under the czars, and the majority of them did not want to support the communist revolt. The revolution was forced upon them by a very small group utilizing "democratic slogans."[3] To be somewhat fair to those who vote for Democrats, their party has been hijacked by a small minority intent on creating a powerful state in the image of Marxism.

Organized Labor

In the late 1800s and first two decades of the 1900s, organized labor grew to enormous size, including millions of men, but excluding women to a great extent, and ethnic minorities almost exclusively. The unions became larger than their employers, but there was no move by the Progressive Era presidents to define them as monopolies and impose limits on their powers. Railroad workers and coal miners' unions were among the most powerful of the day, and they were extremely militant.

During the Great Railway strikes of 1877, unions, often led by anarchists bent on overthrowing the U. S. government, destroyed railroad cars, locomotives, and other assets of the rail companies. More than 100 died in a few days of violence, some of the strikers killed by the militia, but some were simply trying to restore and enforce order. Under the guise of protecting their rights, striking workers found violence an acceptable weapon to wield. Never mind that the destruction of property and commission of murder was criminal. Also, many of the union leaders were criminals in their own self-serving ways. On the eve of World War II, an Associated Press article detailed the historical criminal activity of labor bosses, which included such crimes as "grand larceny, grand theft, felonious assault, white slavery, and extortion."[4]

The violence repeated itself in the Haymarket Riot of 1886, in which strikers hurled bombs at the police and destroyed property owned by McCormick Harvester in Chicago. Death and destruction reared its ugly head again in the 1890s in the Homestead Steel and Pullman strikes. In the latter, Eugene Debs, who would become an avowed communist upon reading *The Manifesto* while in prison, rose to the forefront as a leader of the American Railway Union and the instigator of its support for the Pullman strikers.

By the end of the 1920s, however, those powerful unions had lost some of their luster as workers became disenchanted with paying union dues while seeing little gains in their working conditions. Many were not so keen on the socialist goals espoused by much of the union leadership. Some of the declines were a result of the end of the Progressive Era. The administrations of Warren Harding, Calvin Coolidge, and Herbert Hoover oversaw a return to *laissez faire* policies, a government more likely to side with big business and the allowance of a free market economy in the business world. As the term is used to pertain to business, *laissez faire* means letting the business world operate with little, or no, government interference.

In the final analysis, labor unions are typically socialist organizations. They clamor for what they believe is best for their members, regardless of whether or not it's good for anybody else. In their early days, the unions did have some realistic grievances, such as fair wages, shorter hours, and safer working conditions. Some industries required them to work long hours, sometimes up to 14-hour days, for subsistence pay, and in conditions so dangerous that they could lose arms, legs, eyes, and even their lives. Much of that in the industrial world has been mitigated, often through legislation such as the Occupational Safety and Health Administration, so labor unions have had to create new issues in order to justify their continued existence. But like the communist revolt in Russia, the issues are largely nonexistent until the union leaders, a small percentage of the members, make them an issue. This is where modern labor unions have run amuck with their demands, and sometimes they push so far that their efforts become counterproductive to their own interests. Autoworkers wonder why Americans in increasing numbers buy foreign cars. One reason is that American automobile manufacturers are being forced to price themselves out of the market, mainly because of sharply rising labor costs. Hourly employees in a typical Detroit auto manufacturing plant are being paid 3 to 4 times the wages of the best hourly rate in the oilfield. How can the United Autoworkers expect people who earn 25 to 30 percent of what autoworkers make to be able to afford an exorbitantly priced car? The scenario worsens for those who are earning minimum wage. Meanwhile, the folks in Detroit look around at neighborhoods with growing numbers of empty homes, scratch their heads, and wonder what happened; it was self-inflicted.

Auto manufacturers cannot afford to pay exorbitant wages while their cars languish on sales lots because they are overpriced, so they have implemented several responses to the problem. One solution was to have many of the vehicle's components manufactured in foreign countries to trim labor costs. Also, dealers have been offering financing for absurdly long terms, thus affording lending institutions the opportunity to earn huge dividends on auto loans. There was a time when people could finance a brand-new car and pay the loan off in three years. If a person finances an auto for three years today, they will most likely have a payment that exceeds the mortgage payment on their home. Finally, the manufacturers have sought help from the robotics industry in order to eliminate high labor costs.

The railroad workers' unions, like the auto workers, were pricing themselves out of the job market long ago. Engineers, the people operating the trains, are being paid more than what most oil companies pay a new hire engineer, and the oil company engineer is required to have a formal college degree while the train engineer is not. This is not an argument that operating a train does not require a certain level of intellect and understanding in order to safely move tons of freight from Point A to Point B and do it on schedule, but it's also not rocket science. The train engineers, like the auto workers, don't understand why millions of tons of freight is shipped over the road on trucks instead of on their trains. It costs less, primarily because the railroad workers' unions have made the cost of shipping by rail prohibitive. Railroad companies have also been forced to cut their workforce through innovations in order to remain competitive. The firemen who used to ride in the caboose are no longer needed. Railroads have replaced them and the caboose with a flame sensing device that is attached to the rearmost car. Union workers at Amtrak are the main reason why the rail line operates at a loss every year, and the same is true of the U. S. Postal Service. Amtrak has plenty of competition from the airline industry, and the U. S. Postal Service must compete with FedEx, UPS, and the internet but both Amtrak and the Postal Service have been prevented by their union workforce from making necessary manpower adjustments in an increasingly competitive marketplace. Who pays the ultimate price; in both cases, the American tax payers. When Amtrak or the USPS falls short, as they do every year, the tax payers are forced to ante up so both entities can continue to operate, a condition that cannot endure forever. All tax payers should be able to ride Amtrak or mail a letter without paying a dime because we already pay for those services with our taxes.

Why the discourse on unions, you may ask? It's because unions traditionally support the Democratic Party, and their ideologies are closely in alignment with Marxism. With blinders on, they continually press for exorbitant wages without regard for its impact on the customers they purport to serve. Also, they have become notorious for protecting members from dismissal for drug use and other criminal activity, laziness, excessive absenteeism, and poor job performance. They are convinced that they are the only people that matter, which is basically true of the leadership in the Democratic Party. Power is all that matters to Democrats. Therefore, Democrats/Socialists/Communists will continue to dangle the carrot in front of union members as long as it draws the union vote. When, and if, Democrats seize absolute power, they will toss the unions onto the rubbish heap alongside Hollywood and the lower classes. When Stalin no longer needed the workers to assist him in seizing power, he turned his back on them, paid them a pittance, and watched them die of starvation. The ideologues in the American Democratic Party know that history well, yet seem determined to repeat it, convinced it can work. All of us who don't wear blinders and pontificate self-righteously about what great saviors of the world we will be, are willing to acknowledge that socialism is a failed experiment because it is an inherently flawed system. It chokes itself to death on its own ideology.[5] The chest thumpers in the Democratic Party will not accept that.

The New Deal (or the Raw Deal?)

Every time I hear somebody proclaim that President Franklin Delano Roosevelt ended the Great Depression, my blood pressure rises by at least ten points. There is absolutely no evidence that he ended the worst economic disaster in American history. He was not that smart. To be somewhat fair, I'm not sure anybody at the time was smart enough to end it. In the late 1930s, FDR himself knew that the New Deal had not succeeded, but neither he nor anybody in his "brain trust" wanted to publicly admit failure.[6]

What FDR did do was implement Marx's "industrial armies." Millions of men found employment on works projects such as the Public Works Administration, the Civilian Conservation Corps, the Tennessee Valley Authority, the Rural Electrification Administration, the National Youth Administration, and the Works Progress Administration, to name only a few. Were they paid fair wages by an administration that supposedly believed in fairness? No. Were they paid a wage that significantly improved their standard of living? Not even close. Wages varied from less than $1.00/ day to slightly over $1.00/day. To keep things simple, let's use an average of $1.00/day, which is probably very close to reality. If any of those men who signed on to any one of FDR's socialist armies marching happily off to work volunteered to work 365 days every year, simple math says they made $365 for the entire year. Even in the 1930s that was not much. Also, who wants to work every day of the year? In 1981, during a dual plant startup, I worked a 58-day stretch with no time off, and they were all at least 12-hour days. That's not even close to 365, but I totally lost track of time. I could not tell anybody if it was a Friday or a Tuesday. I didn't know if it was the 3rd of the month or the 23rd. Just getting through another day was all that mattered. I am relating this personal story to illustrate the psychological effects of working that many days without relief. I truly don't know if any of those men during the Depression worked an entire year, but some may have. I do know that we'll never have another generation who would work for so little for so long, and follow that performance by volunteering by the millions to fight a formidable enemy as those men did when they went to war with the Axis powers in the 1940s.

None of the works programs ended the Great Depression. When the nation geared up to go to war against Germany and Japan, and their allies, the country rolled swiftly out of its economic slump. FDR had nothing to do with that other than being a somewhat adequate wartime leader. He also did not win the war; leaders such as Dwight Eisenhower and Chester Nimitz, and the courage of millions of soldiers and sailors, won that war.

Other New Deal programs, such as the Wagner Act, sought to reinforce the right of labor to walk off the job to demand almost anything. The Fair Labor Standards Act established the first federal minimum wage law in the nation's history. Both of these socialist programs dovetail nicely with Marxist doctrine, as both provide government intervention and erosion of the free market system. Democrats have pushed the minimum wage upward, and continue to press for even higher levels without studying the negative consequences, one of which will be the tremendous loss of minimum wage jobs. Some industries, such as the fast-food industry, will have to either lay off thousands of people and/or close numerous stores. You cannot sell hamburgers for $35.00 in a fast-food restaurant because nobody will pay that much for them. While it is true that minimum wage is a difficult level at which to live, it is better than no job. The auto and railroad workers discussed earlier earn much more than minimum wage, but many of them no longer have jobs because corporations have sought ways to reduce their workforce and labor costs.

The Right to Work

When the Declaration of Independence was written in 1776, and the Constitution in 1787, neither document explicitly stated that people have a right to any particular job. However, Democrats, following Marxist principles outlined in Plank 8, are touting right-to-work laws as constitutional. In fact, a lazy person has no right to a job, and nobody should be forced to pay a lazy person good wages for no effective return.

In 1964, President Lyndon Johnson signed into law the Civil Rights Act of 1964, ensuring that persons are not discriminated against in hiring because of race, color, religion, national origin, or gender. Was that a good bill? I will readily agree that it was because discriminatory practices made it especially difficult for minority ethnic groups and women to get a fair chance at employment. But did the Civil Rights Act of 1964 create a fair workplace? Probably not. It's one of the most abused laws in our history. White males who either will not do their job, or take great pains to be a less than satisfactory employee, can be fired with very little documentation as to why, unless, of course, they have union protection. In many cases, those protected by the Civil Rights Act of 1964 can almost literally spend each and every day on the job doing just enough for appearance's sake, and they cannot be fired without a civil rights attorney hauling the employer into a courtroom and suing for exorbitant sums that can make the recalcitrant employee rich and the attorney even richer. This saga has been repeated thousands of times in our courts.

Also, Lyndon Johnson cared little as to the consequences of signing the bill into law. LBJ, an avowed racist who used the 'n' word almost daily, was running for president in 1964 and he would have signed any kind of bill if it assured him the African American vote. He reportedly made the remark that his signing of that bill ensured the African American vote for the Democratic Party in perpetuity; he was using the carrot and the mule trick. Once the legislation became law, he was no longer concerned as to whether or not any ethnic minorities were gainfully employed.

Which party was the true champion of the Civil Rights Act of 1964? Not those racists, like LBJ, who still make up a large cross-section of the Democratic Party. Without overwhelming support from the Republican Party, the bill never would have reached Johnson's desk. Republicans, blinded by their own ambitions, unwittingly elected Johnson in 1964. The fallout continues to this day.

Most who are protected by the bill have the identical mindset of the workforce in the Soviet Union. The "industrial armies" of Lenin and Stalin had no incentive to satisfactorily perform on the job. The state required their services and would not fire them unless they were fomenting rebellion against the state. Our "industrial armies" in the United States know that they can do what they wish on the job and not get fired if they are protected by unions or by the Civil Rights Act of 1964. That bill is one of several reasons explaining why productivity went flat in the stagflation era of the 1970s. A new generation was guaranteed work regardless of whether or not they would perform the duties required by their employer.

Affirmative Action

Affirmative Action is a government requirement implemented in order to "remedy discriminatory practices in hiring" minorities.[7] Its intent, then, is to allow everybody equal access to jobs, essentially what the Civil Rights Act of 1964 was supposed to have done. But it inadvertently turned the tables on both whites and minorities.

Employers began to set quotas, believing that was the intent of 'affirmative action;' a certain percentage of African Americans, a certain percentage of Hispanics, a percentage of Asian Americans, etc., based on the demographics of specified regions. Universities and colleges implemented the same practices for admission to their schools, especially medical and law schools. By this very act they were discriminating against everybody, regardless of ethnicity.

As a hypothetical example, let's suppose that XYZ University was going to ensure that its incoming freshman class would be made up of 17.5 percent African Americans because that was the percentage of African Americans in their region of the United States according to the latest census. Now let's suppose that 25 percent of the applicants who met all qualifications for entrance into XYZ were African Americans, but if they allowed all of them entrance, then the percentage would be above 17.5. By the school's very own policy, the university would be excluding some qualified African Americans. This did, in fact, happen in some cases, but it also excluded qualified white persons who would have otherwise been admitted.

One such person was Allan Bakke, a former marine and a well-educated man who met all the qualifications to get into the University of California-Davis medical school, but was excluded by a quota system very similar to the one described in the previous paragraph. The university allowed 100 new candidates into each medical school class, 16 of whom had to be minorities. Allan Bakke made the cut; he was in the top 100. However, in order to meet their quota of minorities, Bakke was bumped from the class. He then filed suit against the University of California system's Board of Regents and the case, *Bakke v. University of California Board of Regents*, reached the Supreme Court of the United States.

Bakke won his case, but in a very close 5-4 decision. Four justices obviously were convinced that discrimination is okay as long as it is directed at whites, and qualifications be damned. The majority opinion did not necessarily state that 'affirmative action' was a constitutional problem, but they held issue with creating quota systems based on race which they ruled effectively instituted yet another discriminatory practice.[8] At least in this case, five members of the highest court in the land recognized that the utopian/communist system of "equal liability of all to labor" was not only not practical or fair, but government institutions should not be implementing such systems.

Meanwhile, enough Californians saw issue with their state's laws on affirmative action that they were able to place a state constitutional amendment on the ballot in 1996, Proposition 209, challenging state laws on affirmative action. Proposition 209 passed by a vote of 55% for and 45% against, specifically prohibiting public institutions from "discriminating on the basis of race, sex, or ethnicity."[9] Sound familiar? It should because it is almost identical to the Civil Rights Act of 1964. Indeed, it does state the same thing. How many times must legislators repeat themselves in their desperate attempts to create an elusive utopian society?

Why are Democrats, often with the help of Republicans, trying to force Plank 8 of *The Communist Manifesto* on the laboring classes? For the same reasons that Karl Marx wrote that provision into his grossly erroneous ideological diatribe; so the state could dress us all alike and march us cheerfully off to work each morning; so that each and every one of us would become good communists, beholden to the state for our every need.[10]

Marx did not seem to have a good understanding of human nature. He should have studied world history more closely, or perhaps sociology. Slaves or serfs or peasants throughout history have detested their conditions. It robs them of their freedom, a basic human right; it robs them of individuality of purpose; it steals from them the necessary incentive to be proud of their accomplishments at the end of each day. Marx's "armies" would be nothing more than armies of slaves, and not in any racial sense of the word. It would be a condition imposed on the working class that would be politically expedient in order for those in power to exercise complete control over the masses. The American Democratic Party leadership fully understands this Marxist concept, and would like to implement it because it fits with their policy of the destruction of the middle class; make the middle class a massive army of peasant serfs. The specter of the Middle Ages hovers over our existence as a nation of free people.

Chapter Eleven

SCATTER 'EM ALL OVER THE PLACE SO THEY CANNOT ORGANIZE REVOLT

Perhaps Karl Marx and Friedrich Engels were nothing more than ideologues, but it is well known that they harbored a tremendous level of hostility toward the industrializing world, therefore they understood that many of the working class were also angry. They also knew that industrialists and their facilities typically occupied cities, so the Marxist scheme to keep them suppressed was to remove them from their enclaves without arousing suspicion, and then keep them away from cities in order to remain in power. Thus Plank 9: "Combination of agriculture and manufacturing industries; gradual abolition of the distinction between town and country, by a more equable distribution of the population over the country."[1] Cities would be eliminated.

It should be obvious that Plank 9 is most assuredly the pipe dream of ideologues; everybody can live in a little slice of the country. How nice that would be if it were possible, and even nicer if their slice of the countryside was not a frozen gulag. At the time that *The Manifesto* was written, the world's population was approximately 1.2 billion people, and the largest cities in the Western world were approaching 1 million. The global population has now surpassed 7 billion,[2] and many cities are well over 10 million. Even if the very idea seemed grand in the mid-1800s, it was still impractical unless we forced the world to return to the hunter-gatherer systems of prehistoric humans. It's even more impractical today, especially when ideologues like Robert Redford, a good socialist, is not about to relinquish his piece of heaven on earth, his spacious ranches in Montana or Colorado, or wherever he goes to enjoy nature while the rest of us do real work. As all good socialists believe, especially wealthy socialists, everybody should share one another's possessions, just not their own.

But that's not the point that Marx was trying to emphasize. The point once again boils down to controlling the population, and what better way to control them than to force them to abandon the cities and scatter them around the countryside, making it more difficult for them to present a united front against socialist intrusions. Marx could not possibly have envisioned cities of up to 7 or 8 or 10 million people, and even more. The idea would have frightened him. How best to control so many huge cities with millions of people streaming to and from work and pleasurable pursuits on a daily basis, Marx would have wondered. Also, he never seemed to realize that he would be diluting the pool of industrial workers by placing them impossible distances from factories. Plank 9 was a waste of ink, as is the entirety of *The Manifesto*, the bible of the Democratic Party elite.

The Reorganization of America

Richard Nixon, a Republican president, must have been somewhat Marxist because he and his henchmen dreamed up the perfect scheme to accomplish Plank 9 without too much fanfare. Of course, his dreadful plan was never implemented on a large scale, but it very closely resembled the division of the South into five military districts after the American Civil War. During Reconstruction, a ten-to-twelve-year period after the Civil War, the 11 Southern states that had formed the Confederacy completely and totally relinquished all authority to the federal government. It's important to inform readers that this IS NOT what Abraham Lincoln wanted. He viewed the long, bloody war as enough punishment dealt out to both sides in the debacle. We know that he was assassinated, and his plans were shoved aside for the Radical Republicans who wanted to further punish the South as if Generals Sherman and Sheridan had not done enough. In the end Reconstruction failed in so many ways, not the least of which was that it forced the South to submit to military occupation, an act that only served to greatly anger white southerners who were already stinging from defeat on the battlefield. Violent retaliation by the "southern redeemers" would become the legacy of Reconstruction, wreaking havoc on the lives of African Americans for at least another century.

Nixon's Reorganization Plan divided the United States into 10 districts and placed control of most activity in the hands of the federal government. Of course, the plan was, and is, contingent on several factors involving emergency situations.[3] While some on this planet seem to believe that many of these emergencies are going to be, or already have been, instigated by the government as a pretext to implement the complete restructuring of the United States, I am not quite that paranoid.[4] At least, not yet.

However, Americans should know that the plan is a possibility, and given the right set of circumstances coupled with corrupt leadership with a thirst for power, we could find ourselves no longer governed by our fifty sovereign states, and much of Plank 9 would become a reality. Cities would be emptied into the country, which would be a total disaster. Redford might discover several thousand homeless Americans wandering around aimlessly on his private little paradise. Other Hollywood socialists might wonder why they are being forced out of their mansions in Beverly Hills.

Prelude to Nixon's Plan

Richard Nixon had a template to follow for his Reorganization program. It was the work of a Democrat, FDR's successor, Harry S. Truman. He developed the Reorganization Plan No. 7 of 1949, less than four years after the end of World War II. While Truman's plan was milder in form and substance than that of Nixon's, it still contained the nucleus of a plan to seize absolute power at the federal level, abolishing all the powers of the autonomous states.[5] In fact, the 10th Amendment would no longer be applicable.

Truman's gravest concern was the threat of Soviet dominance, which was at the height of its power in the post-World War II era. Their leaders, beginning with Lenin, often touted the spread of communism throughout the world, with the USSR as the supreme power holding sway over the industrialized nations of the globe.[6] Truman was certain he wanted none of that. If anybody was going to rule the entire world, it would be him and his chums in the Democratic Party of the United States of America, or whatever we would be called if such a monstrosity is ever foisted upon the earth's populace.

When the Roman Empire had at last defeated the Jews around 70 AD, they issued them an ultimatum; get lost! The event is referenced in history as the Jewish Diaspora, a forced migration from their homeland that is long forgotten in world history. Many people, among them Barack Obama, seem to think the Jews should not have a homeland in Israel. Before the Diaspora, the Jews co-existed, although not always peaceably, with the nearby Arab world, and had done so for thousands of years, yet there are those who would deny them the opportunity to return to the land of their ancestral heritage. Their forced migration had disastrous results. They were ultimately blamed for the plague in Europe; the Jews had poisoned the water wells. Hitler blamed them for the economic depression of the 1930s, and proceeded to kill as many of them as possible in an effort to create his master race. Stalin, too, can count millions of Jews among the millions of Russian citizens he had murdered. Stalin's numbers almost make Hitler look like a Cub Scout, but "Uncle Joe," as we have seen, was the darling of the Hollywood 10 and President Roosevelt. So, let's implement Plank 9 anyway, because we know it will work; at least Marx said it would. Let's force millions of people all over the world to abandon their homes and jobs in the cities and take them to the country. They would have no place to go, no food to eat, and no jobs. And, like the Jews of forgotten history, they would be murdered, but this time the slaughter will not be a few million or six million. The massacre will be in the hundreds of millions.

It should be obvious to the reader at this point that communism, or statism or utopianism are the ideologies of death, and I must remind you that socialism and communism are the same things. The destruction of the farming industry (Plank 8), along with forced migration instituted by Plank 9, will result in a death toll on unprecedented levels in global history. The Soviets put this into practice by banishing their own citizens to Siberia, where the vast majority disappeared forever. Where will America's Siberia be located? Perhaps somewhere in the one billion acres of land confiscated by numerous presidents? Perhaps in the hinterlands of the Arctic National Wildlife Refuge to freeze to death, or be consumed by polar bears?

No Borders

Have you heard of the folks who propose that one day we will be one world and there will be no borders at all? Democrats actually believe that that ideological disaster can be achieved. Also, they seem to possess the notion that the United Nations somehow was ordained to rule the world as one government. This is pure Marxist thought. While not explicitly stated in Plank 9, Karl Marx did advocate the abolition of borders within the text of *The Manifesto*. He proclaimed that "workingmen have no country," and that as communism develops, the world will see the demise of "national differences and antagonisms between peoples." According to Marx and Engels, the natural order of things will witness the end of "the exploitation of one nation by another" as well as "the antagonism between classes within the nation." Finally, they issue the *coup de grace*; they describe a wonderful world that will exist when "the hostility of one nation to another" is no longer prevalent.[7] All poppycock and grossly impractical.

All of us want an end to wars, but practical considerations easily illustrate the impractical nature of these Marxist proclamations. Cultural differences abound aplenty, and no amount of force can erase the tensions they cause and will continue to cause. After all, in order to do this, we would have to do one of two things: Abolish all cultures as Mao attempted to do in China with his Cultural Revolution, an attempt to eliminate all Chinese cultural connections with their past, including the ancient philosophies of Confucianism;[8] or we would be forced to allow one culture to become dominant globally. Human nature dictates that there would be wholesale resistance to either of these options, and the only way to ward off resistance would be to brutally crush it. But then, the ideologies of death have no problem with murdering people.

Meanwhile, the United Nations, with the acquiescence of the American Democratic Party, continues to pretend that it has global authority. Not a single mandate of the UN is binding on any nation, nor do they have any authority to force their will on any nation. But the "One World" proponents seemingly believe the UN is already the ruler of the world. Marx would have been proud to see that organization forcing his ideology on the entire world. In the final analysis, there is a "clear and present danger"[9] that this could happen.

If it does, it will not only destroy America and its Constitution, but the entire world will erupt in flames. World War II made World War I seem like a walk in the park. Approximately 50 nations were engaged in the first 'global' conflict, and approximately 10.5 million people died. World War II engaged about 80 nations with 55 million deaths. A third global conflict would likely involve every single one of the approximately 180 nations on the planet to varying degrees. In the first two World Wars, there was a clear winner and a clear loser. No such thing will occur in the aftermath of a third global conflagration for a couple of reasons: First, the death and destruction will be of such a magnitude that all nations will be rendered nonfunctional; second, the lines between factions will be so completely blurred that nobody will know who the enemy is. It will be like the French Revolution on a massive scale.

The UN was designed to promote a peaceful world. While that institution may be doing a decent job of reaching the third world with food and medicine, it has not done a very good job of its original charter; keeping the peace. Numerous wars on a small scale have flared up all over the world since the UN was chartered. Instead of being proactive in preventing them, the UN gets involved after the fighting begins. What makes anybody believe that organization is capable of forestalling the destruction of the world?

On economic issues, the UN often attempts to usurp the autonomy of the individual nations. Plank 9 seems to be their mandate. They already view themselves as a duly appointed governing body even though not a single one of them was elected to serve. Since they are not elected officials, then a basic tenet of democracy sorely lacks in their charter. This is not a problem for Democrats, who don't much like democracy anyway.

Chapter Twelve

WE MUST BRAINWASH THEM

How does a manufacturer market its product? Mostly through advertising, telling people what is so great about their product that they simply cannot be without it. Sometimes the commercials are stretching the truth a little, sometimes they are outright ridiculous in their claims to have the greatest product on the market. Communists had to do the same thing, and the USSR was very good at it. So is the Democratic Party in America. What institution did the Soviets use, and the Democrats have been using, to sell statist/socialist notions, or to convince the general population that the state is our greatest benefactor? The obvious answer is our schools, from Pre-Kindergarten all the way through doctoral programs.

This is Plank 10 of *The Manifesto*, the last, but by no means the least of them. It is actually the supporting mechanism, the foundation from which all else springs. Brainwash the children so when they are grown adults, they believe that socialism is the "cat's meow," the "greatest thing since sliced bread," the "saving grace" of the human race. Plank 10 is as follows: "Free education for all children in public schools. Abolition of children's factory labor in its present form. Combination of education with industrial production, etc., etc."[1] I am not certain what Marx and Engels meant by "etc., etc." Maybe they simply exhausted all of their dysfunctional thought processes and plugged in those abbreviations for others to add their own brand of insanity. Perhaps they meant to rehash the rest of the other nine planks of their road map to utopia, to the worker's paradise, but were simply too lazy to type them onto the page again.

We'll explore the first phrase of the first sentence first; "Free education." Anybody who is convinced that education is free is living the great socialist pipe dream. It is not free, and it has never been free. Somebody has to pay for it. All of us are forced to pay a tax in some form in order to support public education. In Texas, it's primarily a property tax. We even have to pay when we do not have any children attending a school. Single persons with no children, pay. Married couples who have not had their first child, pay. Elderly couples whose children have long since graduated from high school or college, pay. Unfortunately, we often do not get the product that we pay for. I protest that my tax dollars in Texas are being spent to teach children doctrines and pseudoscience that I wholeheartedly disagree with.

Does anybody remember enduring the ridiculous proclamation of Hillary Clinton in the Election of 2016: "Free college education for everybody."[2] Millions of Americans must have bought into this nonsense because they voted for her. Those same millions never realized she was pushing for a further extension of Plank 10 of *The Communist Manifesto*. But she's not a communist, her supporters would say, she's a socialist. Remember, it's the same thing. Look it up in a dictionary. Or just examine its platform closely. They are the same. Nobody can deny that her "free college" malarkey is none other than Plank 10. One must wonder how she was going to finance her "free education," a little detail she never truly addressed. It does not take a genius to understand that she fully intended to heap additional taxes on all of us, but especially on the middle class, to pay for her "free education." After one of the pseudo-debates during the 2016 campaign, Hillary made a comment to the press stating that "the middle class needs a raise." I cringed when I heard those words because I knew what she really meant to say was she intended to "raise" our taxes, not our income.

At this point, I will argue that higher education is not a right or a privilege. It's a choice one makes only if that's what they want. If it's what they want, then they should pay for it, not the taxpayers. Oh, wait a minute, take a look at the recipients of your state's disbursements. Tax payers are already paying a huge piece of the higher education pie! Socialists/communists in America have been enforcing Plank 10 for decades, funneling billions into the coffers of colleges and universities and dictating to them what they can and cannot teach. However, Hillary Clinton just wanted to dip her grubby fingers deeper into the taxpayers' pocketbooks, and in reality, most of the additional taxes would never have paid for college, just as the added taxes imposed by the Abominable Care Act do not pay for health care; the money would have simply disappeared into black holes in the government's treasury, never to be seen again at work for the people that paid them. We still don't know where all of the trillions Obama spent ended up!

Hillary Clinton also wants to tell colleges what to teach. Communists have this system honed to perfection. In America, they will hand out tax dollars, and then mandate the ideologies to be taught at universities under threat of losing funding if they do not comply. That is the balance of Plank 10, where the brainwashing of children in the industrial state comes into play. It works exactly like a protection racket operated by organized crime. There are millions in America who believe our government, and the politicians who run it, are nothing less than an elected crime syndicate, stealing from us without restraint or conscience.

What is the patented answer of politicians, especially Democrats, to solve any major problem that arises; pump more tax payer's money into the problem. So goes the mantra in the realm of education. Beginning with the countercultural revolution of the 1960s, our schools and our students have been the victim of declining performance levels, and the only response seems to always be to feed more money into the flames. This has been the cycle for about half a century, but the massive increases in funding have had NO effect on performance. If anything, the downward spiral continues to this day, reaching precipitous levels.

Meanwhile, the rallying cry at the federal level comes from the Secretary of Education and his/her communist organization, the Department of Education. Both are working tirelessly to wrest complete control of all educational institutions, from kindergarten through the doctoral level, away from the states. And they are succeeding by making threats that they will withhold federal funds if performance levels are not met, or if schools are not teaching what the DOE mandates. Meanwhile, we are churning out millions of pages of textbooks that are biased to the very core in favor of left-wing doctrine, all deliberately designed to discredit the intelligence of our nation's founders and the Constitution under which we are governed. Those bent on this venture are committing treason, and they have absolutely no credible plan with which to replace the Constitution. We will be subjects of tyranny if they succeed.

The world of psychology has been an important factor in eroding performance levels in our schools by placing all blame on teachers. Students, according to modern psychology, never misbehave. The student's inability to behave properly and respectfully is not the student's fault, it's the teacher's shortcomings, or it's a host of learning disabilities that once never existed. By the way, it seems that disrespect is not bad behavior after all. The leftists have created this environment in order to utilize it to their full advantage; in order to control the educational institutions and what is presented as truth in the classroom. Those students who misbehave will be the most surprised if the state ever does take complete control of our education, because their punishment will be far more severe than what students of the past suffered. It will be off to the Gulag for them.

- - -

Here's just some of what the leftists want taught with our money:

1. **All men are bad**, especially the founders of the United States, and most especially those who were slave owners. They attack Thomas Jefferson, one of the most intelligent presidents in our history, with vigor. They disregard the fact that while serving in the Virginia House of Burgesses, Jefferson made several attempts to make it easy to manumit slaves in Virginia. They misrepresent his work on the Declaration of Independence. He was overruled when he tried to include language recognizing that people should not be held as property. When he was involved in the writing of the Constitution in 1787, but only as a long-distance adviser, Jefferson, along with many others, was convinced that slavery would die out if they could only contain it to the agricultural regions in the South for the time being. Even Abraham Lincoln, the Great Emancipator and a much smarter man than any socialist today, recognized Jefferson as an abolitionist who pre-dated the movement's rise to the forefront of politics in the mid-1800s.[3]

2. **The Classical Era is Evil**. Greek and Roman literature, art, and architecture were primarily the work of males, therefore, none of it contains

any semblance of validity when studying the classical period. What's left to study? Modern Psychology?

3. **The Renaissance is Evil**, too. For the same reason, the works of Shakespeare, and all his male cohorts in literature, art, or music, portray nothing more than male bias, therefore their work is of no value. I'm not sure what English Lit majors study in lieu of.

4. **Selfishness**. Unlike what John Kennedy said, "Ask not what your country can do for you, but what you can do for your country," the statists teach the young to hold out their hands to see what the government can do for them. A strong work ethic is overrated. If the state can control all wealth, then a person's basic needs will be granted. Tell that to the millions who starved to death when Stalin collectivized the farms in the USSR. What happened to their basic need to eat?

5. **Everybody should contribute their fair share**.[4] Nobody really knows what "fair share" means. Is what is fair to one person, fair to another? If a man doesn't want to work, should he get what a hard worker gets? The Constitution doesn't guarantee equal distribution of wealth, but Marxists believe it should. When the communists seized power in Russia, China, Cuba, Venezuela, North Korea, Vietnam, and other places, did everybody get their "fair share?" Those of us with common sense know the answer is "no." Those who are blinded by communist doctrine want to argue that the answer is "yes." I refer anew to those who starved to death in the USSR. What happened to their "fair share?" Life itself is inherently unfair. We cannot legislate or otherwise force fairness onto society because no system, but most especially communism, is ever going to be absolutely fair.

\- - -

China's Great Proletarian Cultural Revolution is the model for all of the ideas just discussed. Mao recruited youths into what was called the Red Guards. With a vengeance, these young people set about destroying China's past specifically, and world history in general. It was forbidden for the Chinese to know anything of Western culture. Torture, followed by a merciful death, was employed by the Red Guards. The works of Mao became the educational tools, and thousands were murdered in an "anti-intellectual frenzy."[5] Even Confucianism, a philosophy with tenets very closely related to the ideas embedded in Christianity, Judaism, Hinduism, and Buddhism, was forbidden. China's greatest philosophers were symbolically buried, in much the same fashion that liberal intellectuals wish to destroy the great thinkers of the Renaissance and the Enlightenment.

There are other things the school systems are teaching that will be addressed in the following chapters. For now, suffice it to say that the last half-century has witnessed the transformation of our school systems into a left-wing tool to brainwash the young with poisonous ideologies supporting acquiescence to the state in all details of our daily lives. Its effects can be most readily seen in the millennials because they are the most recent demographic to be subjected to the torrent of falsehoods, and at a time when communist doctrines have become well-entrenched in education. The X, Y, and Z generations were not subjected to such hardcore ideological implants, so there seems to be a mix of believers and non-believers among them, but their children will be exposed to increasing levels of Marxist hogwash.

Before leaving the subject of education, I am compelled to address the college professors, especially those in the social sciences who are adherents of communism. These have become a protected species. Conservative professors of history are few and far between, but it's because public universities refuse to hire them. The conservatives will not teach the rubbish that the socialists in the government wish for them to teach. The federal government can threaten the universities with a loss of funds if they are found to be teaching ideologies that do not mesh with socialism/communism.

Meanwhile, the leftist professors can spew forth all kinds of real or imagined and dangerous doctrines without fear of losing their jobs, and when they become tenured, they cannot be fired no matter what they teach or how well they teach it. These are the people who are teaching revisionist history in order to undo the greatest democracy in the history of the world. They know they can never force socialist/communist drivel on an unsuspecting populace if their audience is clinging to the notion that the United States is, in fact, the greatest democracy in the history of the world, so they must destroy that notion posthaste.

One final question: Why do I have to pay taxes that pay the salaries of professors who are espousing what I consider to be rubbish? I demand a full refund.

Chapter Thirteen

FEARMONGERING, AND OTHER LEFT-WING TACTICS

As evidenced by the election of George W. Bush in 2000 and 2004 and Trump's defeat of Hillary Clinton in 2016, the carrot and the mule trick does not always work, therefore Democrats have invented lots of issues that are really non-issues in order to apply pressure on the voters. One of their tactics is to create a "state of fear." While Michael Crichton's book of that title is a work of fiction, it is filled with real graphs of weather conditions that refute the so-called "climate change" nonsense, and the story is really about how the state can use fear tactics in order to convince the constituency to grant them absolute power so they can save us from calamity.[1] Hitler employed the same method to seize power in Germany when he convinced President Paul von Hindenburg that communists were attempting to seize the Reichstag and that he, Hitler, should be made Chancellor and given control of the army in order to restore order. There was no communist move to overthrow the government of Germany, but Hitler got what he wanted. When the smoke cleared, he held absolute power in Germany.

I state unequivocally that the Democratic Party wants as much power over us as they can possibly muster. But they have a problem in our democracy; they have to walk on eggshells lest somebody accuse them of violating the Constitution. Stated otherwise, they have to appear to be abiding by the Constitution, although I have illustrated that they do not. They cannot overthrow our government like the Provisional government did in Russia in 1917 when they ousted Czar Nicholas II, the last Czar and the end of the 300-year reign of the dysfunctional Romanov family, although the Hollywood 10 had no problem with promoting the violent overthrow of our government, as the communists did the czars.

By the end of 1917, the Provisional government was being challenged by I. V. Lenin and his army of Red communists. After a couple of years of bloody warfare between the Reds and the Whites (the Provisionals), Lenin's communist faction (the Reds) prevailed, instituting 70 years of terror in the Union of Soviet Socialist Republics.[2]

Democrats have stopped short of insurrection, although they seem to be subtly encouraging the masses to revolt, as evidenced by the rioting after Donald Trump won the election in 2016. Also, Bernie Sanders has been bold enough to suggest we shred the Constitution of the United States, referring to it as an embarrassment and a document that lent wholehearted support to slavery. Sanders is just another rich politician who doesn't understand the Constitution, nor the mindset of the people engaged in the arguments that went into its composition. It IS NOT a document supporting slavery. It's just the opposite. And Sanders never says what he would implement in place of our Constitution. That alone should raise a number of serious questions in the minds of the electorate about the intentions of the Democratic Party elite.

Many at the constitutional convention pose monumental arguments against protecting the institution of slavery, or even including the word slavery in Constitution. Frederick Douglass, who knew slavery firsthand and who was a much smarter man than Bernie Sanders, agreed with the first statement of this paragraph. The Second Continental Congress, as part of the Great Compromise (the Constitution), banned slavery in the territory north of the Ohio River. A majority of the men present when this ordinance was passed, among them James Madison, another slave owner, viewed the ban as the beginning of the end of slavery, and many of the slaveholders in the upper South had no problem with that concept. Unfortunately, none of those present at the constitutional convention could foresee the entrenchment of slavery brought about by the invention of the cotton gin about a decade later. Abraham Lincoln, another man who was smarter than Sanders, agreed with Douglass' evaluation of the Constitution as a document that would erode the institution of slavery so it would eventually die without government intervention. Unfortunately for Lincoln, he was on the tail end of the time continuum of the abolitionist movement, and he would be the president forced by circumstances to preside over the violent demise of slavery.[3]

What does a child sometimes do if he/she doesn't get his/her way when they want to play with a specific toy? The object (the toy) becomes a target of their wrath and they seek to destroy it so nobody else can play with it. Sanders, as well as others in the Democratic Party, behaving childishly, wish to destroy the Constitution because the voters won't let them have their way. In this case, the toy they seek is absolute power, Constitution be damned. Since Democrats cannot shred the Constitution, which would be treasonous, they resort to other strategies in order to erode the people's confidence in any government other than one of their own making.

Universal Health Care

A part of the Democratic Party platform is universal health care, meaning essentially that the government should operate the health care industry. Under Barack Obama, they came very close to accomplishing their goal of total control of the health industry, but cold feet on the part of some Democrats helped Americans dodge that bullet to some degree, but they still pushed through a bill that made millions of Americans believe they were saved; the carrot was dangled in front of the voters, still just out of arm's reach.

Before the passage of that abominable piece of tax legislation, I argued with a Democrat, basically taking the position that we already had Medicare and Medicaid; why did we need something else? The patented response came back that Medicare and Medicaid were not working. Gee, what a revelation . . . government programs that don't work! In that case, let's just pass another one that will not work. The government, especially with the encroachment of statist goals, cannot operate anything efficiently. Medicare and Medicaid have already proved that the government can run the health care systems no better than they can the post office or Amtrak, or any other kind of business. Governments should govern, not operate businesses.

Universal health care is not something invented by Barack Obama. It's been a rallying cry of Democrats for at least a century, and FDR and Harry Truman both insisted that everybody should have access to "adequate" medical services administered by the government.[4] It is quite likely that both those men obtained the notion from Plato's Republic. They also got the idea from Plato that medical care should be denied to the elderly and the critically ill. In Plato's viewpoint, to create a utopia, those who are not fit to live should not be allowed to live, and the state can implement the process of euthanizing them.[5] Rumors that the Abominable Care Act contained language befitting Plato's utopian notion of eliminating the unworthy were true, but that language was quickly altered when word began to leak out to the general public. Doctors may still treat patients if that is the wish of the patient, but they have some latitude to convince patients to forego treatment, and take leave of this world whether or not their condition can be successfully treated with modern medical technology.

The biggest lie in the wake of passage of the (un)Affordable Care Act is that 20 million Americans were now on health care insurance that previously had none. Not so. The proponents of state-sponsored medical care conveniently forget that close to 9 million Americans lost their private coverage as a result of the government's actions,[6] so the net increase in insured persons is possibly 12 to 14 million, not the inflated number of 20 million. However, try to find among us those 12 to 14 million and they are mostly an illusion. I have spoken with several who explored the possibility of buying Abominable Care coverage and they have said the premiums and the deductibles are so outrageous that it is truly "unaffordable."

As the Republican Party continues to try to undo the damage, which it seems they never will because the fearmongers will attack them in the press, the lies grow with increasing audacity. It's like the fisherman who told the guy at the boat dock he had caught a 12" bass. On the way home, he stopped for gas and told a friend of his that he had caught a 16" bass. By the time he got home, he found an uncle had come to visit, and he told the uncle about his 21" bass. When Republicans initiated discussions to repeal Obamacare, the socialist press raised the alarm and began to throw numbers around that had to be as imaginative as that of the lying fisherman. One early article said that 18 million would lose health insurance coverage if the Abominable Care Act was shoved aside.[7] Other pundits, some before Republicans came to power, and others after, proclaimed the magic number of 24 million who would lose health insurance.[8] As the year 2017 progressed, and the alarmed socialists in the press began to think that Republicans were going to get serious about ditching Obamacare, they, like the fisherman, had to grab on to new numbers, increasing the lie to 32 million who would lose health insurance.[9] Where do they get those numbers and why are they all over the charts and growing? It is fearmongering on an extreme level, and they simply pull these numbers out of the air without basis, and increase them at will in order to frighten the general population, turning them against the politicians who are supporting repeal. The numbers are as much a figment of their imaginations as are the gaseous cows that will be discussed in the next chapter. As of this writing, a fourth attempt at the repeal of this monstrous attack on the middle class has failed due to a handful of Senate Republicans who seem bent on destroying Donald Trump out of jealousy that they did not win the Republican nomination for president, or perhaps they fear the fearmongers. In the eyes of their supporters, those Republicans have betrayed them.

As stated earlier, universal health care is not a new platform for Democrats. Once again, I digress in order to pick up the history. William Jefferson Clinton touted it as his platform in the elections of 1992 and 1996. Clinton was unable to deliver because his party never held sway in both houses of Congress. The point I am making here is that Barack Obama simply latched on to an unfulfilled Democratic/Socialist/Communist/Statist Party scheme when he first ran in 2008.

But Obama knew the recent history well, and when Democrats lost both the House and Senate in the midterms of 2010, he and the socialists went into panic mode. They quickly threw together the measure that would steal billions of dollars from the taxpayers, pushed it through Congress and onto Obama's desk, and got it signed before the shift in power in Congress became effective. The bill was about 2,000 pages in length, and not one single Democrat could tell us much of what was in it. We now know it is picking our pockets, and will continue to do so until the monster is stopped.

Republicans, unfortunately for all Americans, are revealing their impotence and we appear to be stuck with this abominable communist legislation for eternity. Republicans cannot even agree on a new bill's provisions, and they are frightened by criticism from the socialist/communist press. Fearmongering is driving our politics. In the final analysis, "most . . . attempts by government to eliminate poverty," or conditions that dovetail with poverty, "have proven very costly and usually counterproductive."[10] This is proof enough that Democrats cannot efficiently operate the health care industry, but that will not stop them from striving to control it completely.

Religion

Religion has always been, and will likely continue to be, one of the most controversial aspects of life on earth. It's also a very complex one, but Karl Marx and Friedrich Engels had a simple solution to the problem . . . get rid of it. Marx abhorred the notion of religions having some higher influence on humanity, but he most especially despised Christianity. In order to implement his "ideal" society, religion had to be abolished. "Communism abolishes eternal truths, it abolishes all religions and all morality." These are the words of Marx. Although they are not found explicitly in his 10 Planks, they are included in *The Manifesto*.[11] Why have Democrats, most of whom are probably Christians, chosen to turn their backs on their own religion, criticizing it *ad nauseum*, and self-righteously?

What religion did Barack Obama ascribe to? Had Obama read Marx and Engels and did he attempt to put any of their anti-religious schemes in place? Obama would never answer these questions because to do so would reveal his antagonism towards Christianity, an attitude that would not have endeared him even to many of those who voted for him. But Obama did subtly, or perhaps not so subtly, attack Christianity. One example was when Obama spoke at Georgetown University. People should know that Georgetown is a Catholic University, therefore it has symbols and characters which include depictions of Jesus Christ and the name of Jesus Christ in various locales about the campus. Frankly, I am surprised that Obama disgraced himself by setting foot on the campus, but he did precede his actions by requesting that the above-mentioned symbols and characters be covered. Brief news blurbs by the liberal press would never say that Obama made the request, but would say the "White House" made it as if their audience was so ignorant that they did not understand it was the same thing as saying the demand came directly from the president.[12] Georgetown University officials should hang their heads in shame that they complied with the "White House" demand. Didn't Peter deny Christ three times in the final hours before his crucifixion? Georgetown University just as readily denied Christ. Also, what gave Obama the right to ask a Christian institution to disavow the core of their beliefs? He clearly violated the 1st Amendment allowing the "free exercise" of religion.

That incident is but one of numerous attacks on Christianity made by Obama. Every move he made seemed to illustrate that he was a strong supporter of Islam, from his snub of Netanyahu to the senseless and needless deaths of four Americans in the attack in Benghazi to the doling out of about 2 billion dollars of taxpayers' money to Iran so they can continue their nuclear weapons development program. By the way, Iran is mining for uranium in Somalia.[13] What does any rational person believe the Iranians are going to do with that stuff? Uranium, after all, is an important part of nuclear weapons development, and we know where the Iranians got the funding for their uranium operations. Obama's act of granting aid and comfort to the enemy is clearly treasonous. Those who don't believe that radical Islam is the enemy of the United States should just ask any radical Muslim.

But the history of religious conflict goes much deeper than Obama's shallow actions.

Democrats who want to destroy Christianity love to point to the Crusades of the 1100s and expound *ad nauseum* (once again) on the horrible things the Christians did to those innocent Muslims. The pundits conveniently overlook the fact that for 5 centuries, from the foundation of Islam in the 600s into the early 1100s, Muslim "crusaders" had been sweeping over the Middle East, across North Africa, and into southern Europe, and even eastward, slaughtering Jews, Christians, Buddhists, and Hindus by the tens of thousands, and conquering their lands. At the time the first Christian Crusade was launched, Islam was threatening to topple the Byzantine Empire, a primarily Christian state, and the Byzantine emperor was begging the pope in Rome for military assistance from European armies. In spite of the Crusades, Islam prevailed over the Byzantines in 1453. What pretext did Muslims have for committing the slaughter of innocents, other than forceful conquest and the fact that their *Koran* allows them to kill anybody who is non-Muslim? Not one civilization had posed a threat to Islam during those five long centuries of death and destruction. The Christian Crusades, which mostly ended in disastrous failure for the Christians, were nothing more than defensive measures taken to check Muslim aggression.

Fast forward to the Tripolitan Wars between the fledgling U. S. Navy and Muslims out of Tripoli on the North African coast. Thomas Jefferson studied the *Koran* during this conflict in order to gain a better understanding as to why Muslims were attacking shipping throughout the Mediterranean Sea, and killing sailors indiscriminately while demanding the ransom of their cargoes. His conclusion: Muslims intend to kill everybody who is not Muslim.[14] That is the goal for millions of Muslims, although possibly not all of them.

Some readers, at this point, are throwing up their hands and shouting that all Muslims don't think like that. Can we be certain? If not all, then how many? Six hundred million, perhaps? Two hundred million? Either figure is daunting. There are 1.2 billion Muslims on the planet, and we truly don't know where all of them stand on the issue.

Others will argue that the Christian Bible, just like the *Koran*, contains passages instructing Christians to murder all non-Christians. The hole in that argument is that by invoking the name of Jesus Christ, the obvious basis for Christianity, the arguer forgets that Jesus never commanded His followers to murder others simply because they would not follow Him. The Old Testament books contain a lot of historical and prophetic works, but Jesus' death and resurrection displaced much of the older teachings. Nowhere does the Bible contain words of Christ ordering His followers to kill those who will not follow Him.

Democrats also argue that the breakup of the Ottoman Empire, an Islamic state, after World War I, was unfair to Muslims, as was the establishment of a Jewish state in Israel after World War II. First of all, the Ottomans had been causing trouble in Europe, once again for 5 centuries beginning in the late 1400s, like their ancestors had from the 600s to the 1100s. The Ottomans made a mistake by choosing to side with Germany and the other Central Powers in the first global conflict, and they paid for their error in judgment by seeing their empire reduced. As for the Jewish homeland, the Jews were simply returning to where they came from before the Romans scattered them throughout Europe. It had been theirs for a few thousand years before Islam existed, and by the middle of the 1900s, they had grown weary of persecution at the hands of Europeans, admittedly Christians, even before Hitler rose to power. Yes, Christians were complicit in the persecution of Jews, but unlike the actions of Muslims today, that has changed for the better.

Since the Supreme Court decision, *Engel v. Vitale* (ironically, the plaintiff's name is very close to that of Marx's coauthor, Engels), Christianity in America has been increasingly under attack. That court decision outlawed prayer in public schools, even though the Constitution does not explicitly state that praying is unconstitutional. The 1st Amendment says, "Congress shall make no law respecting an establishment of religion, or prohibiting the free exercise thereof." By a strict interpretation of those words, "Congress" had not made any law requiring prayer in public schools, yet the liberal Supreme Court of Chief Justice Earl Warren stretched the interpretation to suit the political agenda of the statists, i.e., the Democratic Party. If anything, the Supreme Court, by its adverse decision, was "prohibiting the free exercise" of religion, clearly violating the 1st Amendment. Why Congress cannot "prohibit" religious practices, but the Supreme Court can, defies logic. The vast majority of the taxpayers supporting public schools are still Christian, and they should not be denied the "free exercise" of their religion. Non-Christians could have opted not to participate in public school prayer.

Marxist doctrine dictates that "despotic inroads" must be made on existing institutions. This would include destroying Christianity, and our Constitution.[15] Why do you think Bernie Sanders and others are clamoring for the destruction of the Constitution? It's not an argument as to whether it's a document that supported slavery or otherwise. It's about "despotic inroads" and the implementation of communist dogma in America. They must "sweep away by force"[16] those institutions that represent true freedom of will and expression. The 1st Amendment is an impediment to their goals, while at the same time, they love to invoke its ideals on freedom when the mood suits them. Freedom of speech or religion is a right unless a conservative is expressing his/her viewpoint.[17] That's when the Marxists have an issue with our 1st Amendment rights.

The Family

An extension of the attacks on religion is the attacks on the nuclear family. In Plato's utopia, the city-state (the government) "replaces parents" in order to exercise absolute power over the education and welfare of the child.[18] This notion was strongly suggested by Hillary Clinton in several works that she published in the 1970s. She believes that "the state has the right to challenge how a family raises their children." She views the family as a "political institution, subject to state control," therefore the state can make all decisions concerning the child, including what they are taught. Her position shifts parental rights to the state, stripping children of the nurturing of parents.[19] This is fascist, or statist, doctrine. It smacks of mind control because the state, not parents, would raise our children, and therefore teach them only the things the state wants them to know, including the notion that there is no god.

Charles de Montesquieu warned long ago that it would be dangerous for the state to supersede in religion and family "through legal coercion." Good laws are designed to regulate the actions of the citizen.[20] Trying to legislate the morality of humans is, simply put, an intrusion on their natural rights. Our federal laws dive deeper into the educational system with each passing year, and the result is being seen as more and more generations seem to forget the truth about the communist past, and are indoctrinated into the notion that the state should be all-powerful. Hillary Clinton's vision seems to be every single child marching off to class dressed in identical garb and possessing identical thoughts, entirely bereft of parental influences.

Fracking

While continuing to dangle the carrot in front of their constituents, the leftists keep coming up with new fearmongering tactics. One of them is fracking, but not a single journalist or politician who blathers incessantly about the so-called evils of fracking actually knows what the methodology entails. Many of them possess the totally off-the-wall and mistaken notion that a huge explosion occurs underground, setting off all kinds of calamities at the earth's surface. But Democrats are not averse to utilizing myth and false science to try to destroy the economy and seize absolute power in the midst of economic disaster, an example set by FDR, the only president to choose to run for a third and a fourth term because, in his own egotistical estimation, he was the only person capable of leading America through a global war. Fracking is said to cause any of the following: Earthquakes, sinkholes, natural gas seeping into water systems, or other forms of contamination of groundwater. It does none of the above, but the word itself has been utilized to instill fear by lending it sinister connotations.

Journalists, unless they write for the Oil and Gas Journal, have no idea what they are talking about when they discuss matters pertaining to oil and gas production. They don't know what makes oil or gas flow from pockets or zones deep beneath the earth's surface up to the well-head and beyond. They don't even realize that when they discuss the practice of producing those hydrocarbons, they are talking about substances that naturally occur at many depths of the earth, including rare cases right at the earth's surface. Those journalists are spewing hot air faster than a sinking hot-air balloon. They are talking heads who know absolutely nothing about the subject, but pretend that they do and convince their audiences they are authorities on the subject. They are not even close, nor are the comedians who parrot them.

Many wells that are still producing today have never been fracked, but the talking heads on television think all wells have been fracked. Many wells produce from zones with enough sub-surface pressure to force fluids to the surface, or they may be older wells equipped with downhole pumps that are driven by the large horsehead pump jacks at the surface that we see rising up and down as they operate the pump somewhere deep in the ground. These are typically producing from zones that do not require fracking.

Fracking is a scientific method of tertiary recovery of natural gas and crude oil from zones with extremely tight sand formations where the flow of hydrocarbons is extremely limited. These are usually at depths never before exploited in the production of oil and gas, mainly because it is expensive to do so. Fracking is the use of a substance, which can be coarse sand (sand fracking), water, carbon dioxide, or other substances that are essentially harmless to the environment, in order to fracture the formation enough to allow for the free flow of the desired hydrocarbons, be it oil or gas. The fracking substance is simply forced into the formation under high pressure, but there is never an explosion.[21] When a person places a jack under their car to lift it off the ground and remove a tire, the jack moves the car just a few inches, so the tire isn't resting on the ground. In almost all cases, fracking doesn't change the formation as much as a car jack moves a car. It is an extremely slight adjustment in the rock formation in order to create a fissure that will allow the hydrocarbons to flow more freely, and is a very safe method of natural gas and oil extraction.

Fracking does not cause earthquakes. Scientists confirmed long ago that they are caused by the shifting of huge tectonic plates, usually two rock formations that have been resting against one another beneath the earth's surface for thousands of years. Man cannot create, or cause, an earthquake. This phenomenon of nature has been occurring since before the beginnings of recorded history without any subterranean activity induced by humans.

The ancient Indian city-states of Mohenjo-Daro and Harappa are known to have been completely obliterated by earthquakes and severe flooding of the Indus River almost 4500 years ago. In 1690, Jamestown, the capital of Nevis Island and the birthplace of Alexander Hamilton, was "swallowed whole by the sea during an earthquake and tidal wave."[22] In 1906, long before the use of fracking and prior to any large-scale oil production in the region, San Francisco was obliterated by an earthquake. In 60 seconds, the quake started enough fires that about 500 city blocks were burned in just three days.[23] There was certainly no such thing as fracking in ancient India, or in 1690, or in 1906 in California, yet earthquakes were already prevalent and were very violent natural disasters. Historically, there are far more quakes in Asia than on any other continent, but far less fracking there than in North America.[24]

Fracking does not cause sinkholes. Sinkholes occur on the earth's surface and are usually caused by long periods of drought followed by heavy rain. They can also occur naturally with the passage of time. Troughs and peaks formed rivers and mountains thousands of years ago, or so it seems to us. We cannot see the natural changes in the contours of the earth because we are only here for a short period of time relative to the eons it takes to reshape the planet. Fracking occurs deep within the earth, sometimes at 12,000 feet or more, and the ever so slight fissure created in the formation at that depth cannot have such an impact on the surface of the earth as to cause sinkholes.

What the average person doesn't know, and Democrat fearmongers don't want them to know, is that water, oil, and natural gas have been mixing with one another below ground since the beginning of time. This phenomenon is not caused by fracking. When oil and gas are produced, water usually comes up the tubing with the hydrocarbons. Oil companies did not cause that. The water was already present in the formation and it never was water that a person could drink. It is as salty as ocean water. Fresh water tables, in most regions, are much shallower than hydrocarbon zones, and therefore do not communicate with hydrocarbons, explaining why the water is fresh and drinkable, even though it came out of the ground.

However, there are rare instances of oil and gas being very shallow, and oil companies didn't create that phenomenon, either. Stories abound of people poking their index finger, or a cane in one instance, into the ground long before the first major oil well came in at Spindletop, south of Beaumont, and finding oil or gas only inches below the surface. [25]If one attempted to make a water well in that environment, it might well be flammable, but oil companies did not make it so; nature did. The Karankawa Indians of coastal Texas told stories of tar balls washing ashore on the various islands off the coast of Texas. These were created by oil seeping out of the ocean's floor long before Europeans arrived, not by drilling for oil or by fracking the formation. When De Soto was shipwrecked on the upper Texas coast in 1543, his men found "petroleum tar floating on the tide" to use as a sealant in repairing their boat.[26] Native Americans in what became Texas told of "brown fluids" oozing from the ground that they would use for medicinal purposes. Early settlers found this to be true, and would use the substance (we call it crude oil) to grease wagon axles, but some of them found that the stuff was so shallow it mixed with fresh water and made it difficult to dig a well with good, clean, fresh water.[27] All these stories pre-date the rise of the oil industry.

In the final analysis, modern oil companies do far less to harm the environment than fearmongers want us to believe. Oil companies are extremely environmentally conscious, but sometimes an accident happens. However, oil came from the ground; does it really hurt the earth when it is spilled? Used motor oil spilled onto your yard might cause the grass to die off shortly after the spill. However, the following summer, that same spot will have the thickest, dark green grass in the entire yard. Salt water, too, comes from deep within the earth. Why is it so terrible to put it back where it came from utilizing a disposal well? But salt water, unlike oil, will permanently kill grasses at the surface. Thus, the disposal well system is used to return it to the depths from which it came and where it does no harm.

What will be terrifying is the immediate starvation of millions of people if fearmongering Democrats achieve the goal of either destroying the oil industry or taking complete control of it. If we kill the oil companies, other industries will be destroyed with them as well. We take plastic for granted. All kinds of electronic equipment, desktop computers, laptops, televisions, keyboards, smart phones, etc., are filled with plastic components, and the case in which the components are housed is plastic. We use mountains of plastic containers for packaging or storing food. The root source of plastic is ethane and propane, liquefied hydrocarbons produced by oil companies from natural gas deposits. Plastics will no longer exist without oil and gas production. Perhaps we can make computer keyboards from wood or stone? But if we use too much wood, then would the hundreds of millions of acres of untouched forest not be in imminent danger? The Flintstones do, indeed, make lots of stuff from wood and stone, even their televisions, but alas, they are cartoon characters who also use their feet to propel their cars. All ridiculousness aside, we cannot make keyboards from wood or stone, no more than we can sustain a modern lifestyle without hydrocarbons. We cannot return to the horse and buggy days, or worse, the hunter-gatherer era. To do either would doom the human race.

Gun Control

The left-wing media never questions why Democrats want to take all guns from the citizenry. Democrat's claims that it will prevent murders are more utopian pipe dreams. It will not stop killing, but that does not matter because that's not even the real reason the Democratic Party elite wants to disarm Americans. Thomas Jefferson said that citizens should be armed to protect themselves from "the tyranny of the government." Democrats know that they cannot seize absolute power without opposition, and if the opposition is armed, they know they will face huge challenges; there's the truth about gun control. Without our guns, we are at the mercy of a tyrannical government. Jefferson understood this well.

One only has to pay close attention to the hypocrisy of the media to understand why some powerful persons want to disarm the citizenry. An illegal immigrant recently shot four people on the freeways in Austin, Texas. Normally, the media would have never shut up about taking away guns in the aftermath of the shootings. However, the perpetrator was an illegal immigrant, so they were not about to howl too loud because it would lend credence to arguments for better enforcement of immigration laws. On the other hand, some in the media thought the man who interrupted the shooting in the church south of San Antonio should be investigated, stopping just short of accusing him of being an accomplice. The man lived nearby, he owned guns, he heard firing and knew something was wrong, and he grabbed a weapon and chased down the real killer. The idea that a citizen could defend himself against a tyrannical government as well as against a criminal frightens the left-wing media and politicians. Taking away his guns, and those of all other lawful gun owners, is the only way to ensure a government or nation can dominate its citizenry.

There are those who argue that the Second Amendment does not protect individual rights to gun ownership, that only the militia, as referenced in the amendment, are allowed to have guns and they stack those guns in an armory. The question we have to answer is who were the militia? They were individuals. Also, where did they keep their weapons? They hung them on the wall at home. The militia is the people, not the National Guard or the Army Reserve.

Chapter Fourteen

THE CLIMATE CHANGE LIE

This non-issue is the ultimate in fearmongering, a favorite strategy of Democrats/Socialists/ Statists that they have been relentlessly selling for much longer than most people realize. Bernie Sanders, Al Gore, Barack Obama, and others have called climate change the single greatest threat to humans in the 21st century. It is not! Those who support this pseudoscience are likely the greatest threat to the security and freedoms of Americans because there is a very ominous threat behind their carefully veiled words; it is nothing less than a demand for absolute power, a ploy to force Americans to surrender total control of the cherished democracy in which we live to those who will destroy it.

Some may even accuse me of fearmongering when they read this diatribe against the Democratic Party elite, but if one reads this work with an open mind, they will readily understand that the true danger is in the lies told by the left in order to convince us to hand over the keys to power so they can save us from a disaster that is no more real than the communist threat was to the Reichstag in Hitler's Germany in 1933.

Simply put, it boils down to state control of every aspect of our lives, including mind control and population control, ideologies that will entail the deaths of millions, if not billions, of people globally. This discussion of deaths of that magnitude is supported by historical records. We know what happened in the Soviet Union and other communist states. Collectivized farms, the destruction of industrial capacity and ability to utilize natural resources, forced migration, cultural purges, suppression of religion, and other totalitarian dogma have historically been extremely deadly, and there is no reason to think that if we try to impose state control in the United States that deaths will not occur again, only in this instance it will be on a magnitude that far exceeds levels experienced by the Russians and all other communist states. Indeed, the death toll will surpass the sum total of deaths in all communist and fascist nations combined.

Let's explore the history of climate change. As stated, most people, especially those below the age of thirty, seem to think it just came up in the last decade or so, but most people below thirty are more interested in staring at the latest smartphone 24/7 than they are about learning history. All too many above thirty do so as well.

"Climate change" has sported several titles, because as conditions have changed, the perpetrators of this scare tactic have had to take a new approach. It may pre-date the 1960s, but this man-made climate problem was definitely bandied about in the 1960s. However, in that decade, the earth was getting colder. That's right . . . getting colder is exactly what I said. Why was it getting colder? According to the so-called experts of the day on climate change, it was because of increasing volumes of carbon emissions, greenhouse gases, from 1940 to 1970.[1] We were being told that we were going to freeze to death because greenhouse gas emissions were blocking the warmth of the sun's rays. But how can that be possible? The same phenomenon, increasing carbon emissions that once made the earth get colder, is now making the earth grow warmer. What kind of pseudoscience must this be? How can carbon emissions do both? The truth is that they cannot do both because that would be some sort of magical trick of science, like having the sun rise in the west instead of its usual ascendancy from the east, or maybe the earth really is a flat disk, and the moon is really made of green cheese. A more serious example might be that scientists have decided that the closer proximity of the moon actually forces the tides to recede instead of rising.

Invariably the chilling of the earth stopped, as it has done dozens of times in history, and it began to get warmer, so the pseudoscientists (mostly politicians masquerading as scientists) had to change positions. They hit on a real gem; lots of things emitted into the atmosphere, among them Freon, were burning holes in the ozone layer, thus allowing the sun's rays to intensify at the ground level. This was when the pseudoscientists began to use the term "global warming." When it was proved that the holes in the ozone layer have been expanding and contracting unmolested since the beginning of time, the fearmongers, not willing to relinquish their grip on this delightful ruse, simply changed the name of their platform to "climate change."

Their new name, climate change, captures it well because now, no matter whether the earth gets warmer or colder, it's still climate change. If there are 50 hurricanes in a given year, it's climate change. If there are only 6 hurricanes, it is still climate change. Somebody at the elitist level within the Democratic Party had finally hit on a moniker for their strategy to seize power that they will never have to change. Probably the guy who invented the paper clip and the internet. You know him; he was once the nominee of the Democratic Party for president of the United States, and he's never invented anything. Facebook is filled with lots of stuff that the millennials think is real, so the climate change fearmongers use it a lot because that group of younger Americans forms the voters of the future. I recently studied a pair of photos on a Facebook post, one supposedly depicting the climate change "experts." It was a room of mostly men (if not all of them men), and they were dressed to the nines; three-piece suits, immaculate coats and ties, and their hair was combed in perfect parts. They appeared to be paying rapt attention to somebody off-camera who was discussing this dreadful issue, "climate change." The photo next to it, as you may have guessed by now, was supposedly the scientists who opposed the climate change "experts." Nobody was in a coat or tie. Their hair was disheveled. Their posture was slouching and they appeared to be disinterested in their master of ceremonies. I studied both pictures closely for about 10 minutes, and finally used a magnifying glass to get a closer look at the small figures in both scenes. The people in both pictures were in the same room, and they were the same people! At that point my supposition was that the fearmongers had enlisted the aid of a number of people, probably not a single scientist among them, dressed them nicely to pose for the first photo, and then mussed them up for the second. That's how it works, folks; lies, lies, and more lies. It is a well-known fact that if a lie is told often enough, it becomes the truth to those who don't investigate. Even the storytellers will convince themselves they are telling the truth.

The Most Absurd Story of All

One of the most ludicrous "conclusions" of the climate change "experts" has no scientific basis whatsoever. Even a man with a Harvard law degree, Barack Obama, appears to believe the ridiculous notion that cows breaking wind are causing the earth to grow warmer. Not a single shred of scientific data exists to support this insanity, nor does any instrument exist with which we can accurately measure the volume of a cow's fart, much less the impact of the escaping gases on the atmosphere, so the fearmongers must have a more sinister reason for pressing this insanity.[2] They cannot leave the poor cattle alone to relieve their bloated stomachs in the peaceful environs of their pastures.

An examination of the left-wing's set of solutions to the non-issue of flatulent cattle is quite revealing, almost a tacit admission that they don't even believe their ridiculous story. One resolution is to force ranchers to build a structure that will contain cow manure, thus requiring cattlemen to scour thousands of acres in order to collect all of it before it dries, at which point it no longer emits gases. Perhaps the self-righteous chest thumpers in the Democratic Party view the idea as a big outhouse for cows. When the urge strikes, the cattle will hustle over to their very own privy, take care of their business, clean up with the Sears catalogue, and then return to the pasture. This so-called solution is not only impractical, it's cost-prohibitive, which explains why Obama, et al, want to force ranchers to do it. His goal appears to be to destroy the beef and dairy market, reducing our food supply, thus causing the deaths of millions. Democrats, including Barack Obama, do seem compulsively concerned about the world's growing population, but their answer to the issue seems to be to formulate policies resulting in the deaths of a few billion, as opposed to policies that might continue to feed the increasing population.

Yet, at the same time, perhaps Obama, et al, want something else; more of our money. As another solution to gaseous cows, Obama has suggested taxing beef at the supermarket in order to reduce beef consumption. The point I am making here is that, once again, and as is so often the case, new taxes are the solution chosen by Democrats, and all too often even by their brothers in the Republican Party. We have to keep in mind that one of Marx's main goals was the destruction of the middle class. Piling tax upon tax on them will accomplish that. The most important point of this discussion, however, is that this gassy cattle thing is nothing more than a hoax. It is pseudoscience at its worst, and "I am outraged"[3] that people will listen to this drivel from world leaders who are supposedly intelligent human beings.

A History of Severe Weather

The simple truth is that man-made emissions, nor gassy cows, are the cause of any shifts in the atmosphere's temperature or the intensity of storms. During the American Revolution, there were a number of days in which soldiers experienced exposure to excessive heat and/or foul weather. On the march leading up to the Battle of Brandywine, General William Howe's British army was on the move when it was "blisteringly hot, **killing 27 men and 170 horses.**"[4] [emphasis added] Soldiers at the Battle of Monmouth in New Jersey in June 1778 described temperatures in the "nineties" and compared it to the "mouth of a heated oven," and the "intense heat" which made the fighting even worse.[5] Abraham Lincoln spent a few years in the nation's capital as the representative from the state of Illinois. In 1848, he experienced an especially "long, hot summer."[6] July 4, 1850, was described as "hot."[7] These observations were made by men long before the advent of air conditioning, so they were men who were accustomed to the heat of summers. If they were noting them as "hot" or describing a "long, hot summer," then it is reasonable to conclude they were witnessing unusually high temperatures. These are but a few examples of temperature extremes pre-dating the rise in carbon emissions, but it would take volumes to recite all of them. It should be obvious, though, that hot weather is not a novel experience in the history of the world.

Powerful storms are also no more novel than hot weather. In Narragansett Bay in Rhode Island, both the British and the French fleets during the Revolution were battered by "gale force winds" and pounding rain in early August of 1778.[8] Much of Lincoln's life was spent in the state of Illinois, which meant he was in close proximity to the Mississippi River. The first capital of the state, Kaskaskia, had to be moved because of "routine flooding from the Mississippi River."[9] Some writers of the west have averred that "capricious weather" was more dreaded than death at the hands of Indians.[10]

Raging forest fires and grass fires are also touted by leftists as being caused by man-induced changes in the climate, but those disasters, too, are nothing new. "Prairie fires" have been described as the "most common enemy" of settlers in the west in the post-Civil War period. One writer describes "tongues of flame shooting high into the air" and numerous fowl flying high above them, desperately trying to avoid being cooked alive. Thousands of acres were quickly reduced to ash, and the animals on the ground, unlike the birds, were unable to escape the scorching heat.[11]

Pseudoscience Fabrications

One of the biggest lies from the climate change "alarmists" is that 97% of all scientists in the world believe that human activity is causing the world to grow warmer. The 97 % is a bogus number made by the extrapolation of carefully selected numbers in order to achieve the desired outcome. Many of those included in the calculation are not even scientists; they are humanities professors at universities who agree with climate change because it's expedient to do so or face the loss of millions of dollars in grant funding from the government (the taxpayer). In fact, less than half of real scientists agree that climate change is man-made.[12]

In truth, there exists a tremendous level of bias in climate change literature simply because the persons involved in publishing it are filching grant money at exorbitant levels,[13] and much of the source of the data being utilized is not even being shared publicly.[14] Why is the so-called proof of climate change being held in confidence? This cloak of secrecy alone suggests that the information is likely bogus or non-existent, therefore easily challenged. Also, Democrats want us to accept this pseudoscience on the basis of their word, disavowing any opposing arguments.

The Non-Governmental International Panel on Climate Change poses conclusions that are simply ignored by those who choose to support the end-game on climate change, and the liberally biased press fully supports the hoax. In other words, opposing conclusions by real scientists are suppressed. Some of their conclusions that contradict the climate change hoax are as follows: Sea levels are not rising at any more rapid pace than they have for the past century; "droughts have not become more extreme;" there is no "significant increase in the frequency or intensity of storms."[15] Indeed, a hurricane obliterated the small village of Indianola on the Texas coast in 1886. Fourteen years later, in 1900, Galveston was leveled by another severe storm that left 5,000 dead, to date still the worst natural disaster in the history of the United States in terms of the loss of life. Both those storms preceded the false god of climate change. Property losses do continue to grow, but that is a function of the growth of America's coastal cities, which are far larger today than they were 120 years ago.

Another truth about the earth's climate is that warming and cooling trends have occurred in cycles over thousands of years, obviously refuting the clamor that human activity is the cause. As a general rule, the earth has been in a warming trend since the last great Ice Age, some 10,000 years ago. There was a spike in temperatures in the Minoan period in the 1390s B.C., and another in southern Europe around 170 B.C. that is referred to as the "Roman Warming."[16] Those Romans must have had gasoline engines on their chariots and historians have just missed that key piece of information. How else can one explain rising temperatures in classical Rome?

Using climate change pseudoscience as their platform, the Environmental Protection Agency has been imposing coercive regulations on Americans since 1970 when President Richard Nixon illegally created the organization. The Constitution does not grant a president the power to create any government entity. That must come from Congress. However, Congress does not have the constitutional authority to attempt to regulate the weather. Meanwhile, the EPA, like the FBI, has become a totalitarian and tyrannical organization, almost a government within itself, creating illegal regulations (not sanctioned by our elected representatives in Congress) and making criminals of Americans.[17]

Obama Wins an Oscar and Hollywood Weighs In

On June 13, 2013, Barack Hussein Obama delivered a speech at Georgetown University in support of his climate change agenda, including an announcement of the cancellation of the Keystone Pipeline project.

(This was one of the speeches in which he had the university denounce its Christian beliefs.) Throughout the speech, he repeatedly mopped his brow with a handkerchief, as if to underscore how warm it had become in the District of Columbia. What a crock of Hollywood melodramatics! Anybody knowledgeable about that area's history will know that even before the swamp was filled in on which to create the nation's new capital in the 1790s, it was a humid, hot, hell-hole in the summer. The early government even made sure that Congress would adjourn in late spring so that everybody, presidents included, could escape inland to higher altitudes, thus avoiding the insufferable Washington summers. Obama's brow mopping was nothing more than acting. Give the man an Oscar, but his climate change hogwash remains just that…hogwash. Also, the man has never done a day's physical labor out in the hot summer sun in his life. He should try it for the experience.

Early in his first term, Barack Obama launched a "green" program that was supposed to create 5 million new jobs in the green energy industry that would "end our dependence on foreign oil." He immediately began to hand out millions in tax payer's money to companies that were certain to accomplish his impossible goal. In the words of Deroy Murdock, "these doomed projects devoured $3.4 billion in taxpayer funds." Every single one of the companies discussed in Murdock's article from July 2012 went bankrupt because they were providing nothing of value to the consumer. This is a rarely discussed, and seemingly little-known aspect of Obama's first term, but obviously, Deroy Murdock knew what was going on.[18] Obama was quick to blame everybody but himself for this wanton abuse and waste of government funds.[19] The taxpayers deserve an explanation as to what really became of all that money. Remember Andrew Jackson?

Not to be left off the bandwagon, the leftists in Hollywood have to continually remind us that we are doomed. Of course, we all know that these Hollywood geniuses are scientists, too. And pigs do have wings. In 1997, Sebastian Junger published a work of fiction entitled *The Perfect Storm.* Without going into details of the plot, the story is about a fishing boat's crew caught in a terrifying storm at sea. In 2000, Hollywood released a film version of the book starring George Clooney, a self-proclaimed supporter of all liberal causes, but mostly a condescending supporter of any left-wing dogma, setting in motion a new trend in fearmongering. There was no such thing as a "perfect storm" until that movie was released.

The harrowing experiences of the commercial fishing boat's crew were as much fiction as is the politically driven mantra of climate change. Suddenly, scientists and weathermen latched onto this new phrase, using it to describe almost any storm, and touting the notion that this is real science. No definition of a "perfect storm" existed until the advent of the film, then the pseudoscientists, including Hollywood left-wingers, have worked tirelessly to create a definition from nothing. There is still no such thing as a "perfect storm!" What constitutes "perfection"? It does not exist unless you are one of those Hollywood characters that believe they are perfect.

A new release in 2017 was *Geostorm*, which is nothing more than Hollywood propaganda in support of the climate change fearmongers. The story is pure fiction, but many who watch it will come away frightened that it is really going to happen because something sinister is just around the corner and humans are the cause. In the story, the ocean tide rises to ridiculous heights, engulfing skyscrapers that are more than one thousand feet tall, and washing away huge cities in a matter of seconds. I refer you back to Idso, Carter and Singer's conclusions; the oceans are no deeper than they were a hundred years ago. If ocean levels were rising at such "alarming" rates, then Miami and New York, as well as many other coastal cities, would have been obliterated long ago. The message being sent by Hollywood in *Geostorm* is obvious; we are doomed, man is the cause, and we must hand all power to Democrats, so they can save us from ourselves. Never mind that we will be forced to surrender our freedoms in the process.

\- \- \-

We are constantly reminded that each passing year is warmer than the last, but history proves that these proclamations are false. In 1896, a severe heat wave struck the Northeast and the Midwest, leaving behind **1,500 dead.**[20] [Emphasis added] No heat wave since then has been so deadly. A December 1941 edition of the Los Angeles Times recalled a heat wave that swept over the city in 1939, sending thermometer readings well above 100 degrees.[21] Even today, it is rare for Los Angeles to see a thermometer reading above 100, unless a person places the thermometer against a blacktopped asphalt road or buries it in the sand, but doing so is not an accurate method of measuring ambient temperatures. True and accurate temperature measurements should not even be done in direct sunlight, much less on a surface that absorbs and intensifies heat waves.

To sum this up, the Democratic Party elite might not even believe their own pseudoscience of "climate change." Then again, they have lied about it often enough that they may have finally convinced themselves. However, much of this dogma is aimed at efforts to steal more money from Americans, especially middle-class Americans, under the guise of "protecting" the planet. But the real goal, the one they will never admit publicly, is to eventually convince Americans to relinquish their freedoms as the Democratic Party gradually seizes absolute power. Obama's answer to farting cows is to impose a tax on beef at the supermarket. That is not going to resolve this non-issue, and he knows it will not, but that's not what he has in mind. Marx knew the only way to successfully implement communism was to eliminate the middle class. Obama, the Clintons, Bernie Sanders, et al, know this strategy well. How often must we listen to the mantra that larger and more costly government is the answer to all of our imagined problems before we come to the realization that the lie is just a means of access to absolute power? "Climate change" is nothing more than fraudulent politics. To quote Gary Pecquet, "It is also probable that many of the recent ecological scares are scientifically unfounded."[22] It is not about science or saving the planet; it's about the politics of power.

Chapter Fifteen

THE DEATH KNELL OF DEMOCRACY

Ernest Hemingway's novel *For Whom the Bell Tolls* is set in the 1930s during the Spanish Civil War. His main character, Robert Jordan, is an American partisan fighting for the cause of the Republic, but his faction is supported by communist forces from the USSR who are opposing the encroachment of fascism. We know that Generalissimo Francisco Franco's fascists prevailed. At one point in the story, though, Hemingway reveals to the reader his understanding of the Democratic Party in America as one that is promoting communist ideals. Jordan is reminiscing about his grandfather, who had fought in the Union armies during America's civil war, and Jordan wonders what the man would have thought of his affiliation with the communist forces in Spain. He recalls that his grandfather would have never "knowingly sat at a table with a Democrat."[1] Hemingway was an avowed socialist, and this passage in the story reveals to the reader quite clearly that Democrats in the 1930s had already been pressing their socialist/communist agenda. We know that their activities actually date to the Progressive Era (1900-1920) at the least.

There are lots of arguments posed by scholars that the main reason communism did not work in the Soviet Union was that Lenin and Stalin did not implement it precisely as Karl Marx had described, and they believe that if it is implemented as Marx proscribed that it will be successful in promoting the so-called classless, perfect utopia. While it may be true that the revolutionary phase of the transition from czarist tyranny to soviet tyranny did not follow Marxist design, the argument loses validity when one examines it from the standpoint of the 10 planks of communism and how they have been implemented throughout history. Those two brutal dictators implemented all of the planks in the Union of Soviet Socialist Republics almost to the letter, as dictated in *The Manifesto*. The problems that ensued were the direct results of an inherently flawed system, one that relied upon the surrender of basic human freedoms and the installation of totalitarian dictatorships.[2] The problems with communism were not the results of Lenin's and Stalin's own interpretations of Marxist doctrine, but Democrats in America have been subtly mimicking the Soviet example for one hundred years. In fact, Democrats today have begun to refer to themselves as "progressives," resurrecting the term to disguise their true agenda; the wolf is among the sheep.

A brief review of the ten planks is in order at this point. Plank 1 is the abolition of privately owned property, especially land, but including monetary assets and buildings such as homes or factories. The Soviets confiscated all land, vesting ownership in the state. The American Democratic Party, beginning in the Progressive Era with Teddy Roosevelt and lately including the two terms of Obama, has now confiscated about 1 billion acres of land in the United States, some of which could be put to use to serve the needs of the growing population of America. People, not governments, should own land, and 1 billion acres is a massive tract of land. What is the government going to do with all of that property? The answer may prove to be frightening.

Plank 2 is an aggressive and progressive income tax. Josef Stalin, taking the aggressive piece at face value, basically took 100 % of the Russian's money, placing it at the disposal of the state as the state saw fit. A Russian was lucky to have a car, and they were assigned living quarters according to their service to the state. The only persons in the Soviet Union who had any significant monetary assets were the Communist Party elite, the Politburo. Beginning with Presidents Taft and Wilson, the United States has implemented this plank perfectly. Barack Obama, an acolyte of Saul Alinsky and worshipper of a father who basically abandoned him, has stolen billions of dollars through Obamacare, and we have no clue where the money has gone. Dinesh D'Souza said that "Obamacare was a heist with a very big payoff."[3] Obama's father, Barack, Sr., and Saul Alinsky both believed that the state had the right to strip the working class of 100 percent of its hard-earned income.[4] Of course, for Alinsky and Obama, Sr., as well as President Obama, there is no understanding working-class people, because any kind of physical labor, white-collar or blue-collar, was, and is, beyond their comprehension.

In Plank 3, the communist doctrine strips all claims to an inheritance. Marx believed that anybody who benefitted from the largesse of the state should not be able to leave it to an heir when they die. Indeed, Obama feels the same way and his administration attempted to rob more of people's inheritance by implementing exorbitant taxes on them. Planks 2 and 3 have the same goal in mind; 100 percent of all income should belong to the state. Marxism overlooks the fact that people work hard to attain wealth, and the state truly has nothing to do with it. Some will argue that the highways that businesses get to use in order to move their products to markets are built by the state. That argument conveniently overlooks the fact that everybody who uses them pays for the privilege through various taxing schemes.

Plank 4, confiscation of property of emigrants and rebels, was also implemented to the letter by Stalin and his successors, but they had to create criminals in order to implement the idea. This one dove-tails nicely with Plank 1 in that all property becomes the bailiwick of the state. Marx doesn't really detail how it is to be used, but the common misconception is that everybody will get an equal share. Stalin, and other Soviet leaders, had their *dachas* in the country, their quiet estates to which they would escape the turmoil of the city, but masses of people were made into common criminals and shipped off to their worker's paradise in Siberia. The Abominable Care Act does the same thing by criminalizing those who choose not to buy health insurance. Meanwhile, Hollywood figures, who don't plan to part with their wealth, have their country hideaways, but they believe nobody else should have that privilege. Bernie Sanders, who said white people don't know poverty, owns a couple of vacation mansions, either of which could probably house eight or more families comfortably. What a nest of hypocrites!

Plank 5 was also implemented by Stalin, and followed until nearly the end of the Soviet era. All banking was centralized. In that way, the Soviets were able to control exactly how much money the masses had at any given moment. While America does have private banks, and large corporate banks that are publicly held, the Federal Reserve System controls every aspect of their operations. We, like the communists, have centralized banking, and its powers have grown exponentially from the New Deal era through the Obama catastrophe. Communication and transportation, says Plank 6, should be centralized, also. The Communist Party controlled all communication in the USSR. No newspaper, radio, or television station could utter a word without the approval of the state. They even had their official news media, Pravda for newspaper readers and TASS for television viewing. CNN is the official news media of the statists/communists in America. They make up news and pretend it's the truth, and are still desperately trying to prove that Trump stole the election of 2016 with help from the Russians. CNN leapt with joy when Michael Flynn recently admitted he had lied to the FBI about a phone conversation with Russians. What the liberal media refuses to expose is that the phone conversation contained nothing of substance, no proof whatsoever of a conspiracy to enlist the Russians in stealing an election. Most election shenanigans in the history of the United States have been committed by Democrats, from George Parr in South Texas to Huey P. Long in Louisiana, to the big city "machines" in the northeast and Midwest. But the slanted news from CNN mirrors that of Pravda and TASS. Sometimes they go so far as to suggest that Trump is the communist, not the Democrats. Trump obviously supports a capitalist economic structure, thus would never adhere to any communist doctrine. Transportation, too, fell under the control of the government in the USSR. Airlines and railroads were operated by the state, much like Amtrak is in the United States.

Plank 7 is what destroyed the productivity of Russia as it evolved into the Soviet Union. The state seized all factories and farms, leading to the destruction of any incentive to work. Farms failed miserably and millions of Russians starved to death. Factory output decreased because nobody wanted to work diligently if there was no reward system. Obama did seize control of much of the health care industry, and forced General Motors to build a worthless vehicle. Stalin was not subtle in the implementation of Plank 7, but Obama thinks that all Americans did not know what he was up to as he tried to force all of us to become wards of the state; in other words, peasants. Millions of us saw through his thinly veiled communist ideologies.

In Plank 8, Marx described his industrial and agricultural "armies." Stalin implemented this model to the letter, with the results mentioned above in the discussion of Plank 7. There were no performance incentives, so workers revolted against the system by doing less. Franklin Roosevelt instituted "armies" of government employees, just like the ones described in *The Manifesto*, and just like the "armies" in the Soviet Union, they were paid a pittance. Our main army of workers today is the more than 3 million federal employees, bureaucrats who operate with no regard for the Constitution.[5] Unions and unfair laws protect workers in our country who have no desire to do what is required of them on the job.

Plank 9 was implemented in the USSR by creating a virtual dead zone in Siberia. People were arrested, usually for political reasons only, and shuffled off to Siberia, where most of them disappeared forever. This was Stalin's method of destroying the opposition in the population centers where too many people could band together and foment rebellion. Once they were out of sight, Stalin had all public records, birth certificates, diplomas, marriage licenses, etc., destroyed so as to erase any evidence that the person ever existed. As Plank 9 says, distribute the population over the country, an idea that even in Marx's day was ridiculously impractical. What are the statist's plans for the 1 billion acres of land under federal control in the United States? Will most of it become our Siberia?

And then there's the propaganda piece, Plank 10, the creation of "free" schools to spew forth all of this communist gibberish. Schools in the USSR abolished the study of any art, literature, or music that did not originate in Russia. The Beatles were even banned. The history of the world began in 1917, according to Soviet dogma, not 8,000 B.C., or before. Our schools are following the communist model, creating a curriculum that eliminates the study of the works of the Greeks and the Romans, the Renaissance, the Reformation and the Age of Enlightenment. The standard rationale for doing so is all that work was the ideas of men, therefore it has no validity in the world of thought control. The truth is that to undermine the Constitution of the United States, they have to connect its ideals with people they want our students to believe were sinister, evil, and unsavory. Never mind that most of those men, including Washington, Adams, Jefferson, and Madison, were much more intelligent than our leaders are today. Never mind that they created the best democracy in the history of the world. Was it perfect? No, and all of those men willingly admitted it was not, but they also recognized that a perfect democracy entailed some inherent loss of freedoms. Can humans create a perfect democracy? Of course not, as no form of government has ever been, or will be, perfect. However, Bernie Sanders, unlike the realism of the framers of the Constitution, thinks he can create a utopia, which is really communism, and a system that is so imperfect that it poisons and destroys any society that adopts its worthless ideas.

In Chapters 13 and 14, we discussed fearmongering. Another thing Democrats do that begs mentioning is that they resort to name-calling when people disagree with their politics. If you criticize an African American politician, it's only because you are a "racist," not because the person(s) may have supported an idea with which you wholeheartedly disagree, and which has no basis in race. If you don't like Hillary Clinton because you consider many of her actions downright criminal, it's only because you are a male chauvinist pig. If you point out the shortcomings of the Abominable Care Act, it's because you are insensitive to the needs of the poor, even though we all know there are more Americans at the poverty level today than there were when Obama took office. The same notion applies if you try to reduce income taxes, which are illegal anyway. When a person speaks out against the falsehoods of climate change, it's because they don't care about the environment. Never mind that most, if not all, of the venomous notions arising from the climate change fearmongers will lead to the deaths of billions of humans. Banning the use of fertilizers and pesticides, promoting organic farming, and creating state-owned farming operations will be deadly. Absurd notions like that of the farting cows are unbelievably contrived to give the Democratic Party greater power over our very existence. Those with more common sense should be laughing at those who think we can measure the volume of gases emitted by cattle. If anybody ever does invent such a device, we should use it to measure the volume of hot air filling the chambers of the House and the Senate.

Here's one more example of what the false prophets of climate change and statism have wrought on the United States . . . wind-generated electrical power. Most of the cost of constructing the windmill farms comes from the federal government (taxpayers). The person(s) going into the wind farm business risk very little of their own money. Some will argue that the railroads in the 1800s were built largely with federal subsidies. While that is an accurate statement, there is more to the story which is deliberately concealed from Americans. Democrats are very good at telling partial truths to further their agenda. Over time, those railroads that developed in the 19th century managed to repay almost every penny to the government (taxpayers). Those who go into any kind of business with taxpayers' money today, have no intention of ever repaying their ill-gotten booty. As of the end of 2016, the so-called green energy industry had collected the whopping sum of $30 billion in subsidies from the Obama government.[6] The taxpayers will never see a return on that investment.

Returning to the windmills . . . they do very little to produce enough energy to warrant their existence, "supplying less than 1 percent of global energy demand." It would take half a century of building windmills on "every square mile" of a land mass the "size of Russia" just to keep pace with new energy demands.[7] Add to that the fact that the windmills are 300-foot-tall monstrosities that destroy the pristine views of hills, mountains, and prairies. Also, wind farm producers must buy much of the electricity they provide from conventional producers of power, coal, nuclear power, natural gas, and hydroelectric, because wind is not available 24 hours/day for 365 days.[8]

As I was leaving the grocery store some years back, a young lady with a clipboard approached me about switching over to "green" energy. I asked her what the price per kilowatt-hour was, and she quoted a price that was four cents/kilowatt hour higher than what I was paying with my current provider. Her price constituted a 30 percent hike in electrical charges. I replied that wind energy is free and the taxpayers shoulder the burden of installation costs, so how could they justify charging 30 percent more, and she could not respond with anything other than it was healthier for the planet. I have already stated the true reason wind farms charge more for their electricity; they cannot make enough to supply their customers, so they buy electricity from other, more reliable and more stable producers.

Battery-powered vehicles are one of the most wasteful vehicles invented, but the liberal press will never admit that fact. Pound for pound, the energy consumed by battery-operated vehicles far exceeds the energy in gasoline. One source gives this example: "A mid-sized auto can travel 30 miles on one gallon of gasoline," while an electric car, "using the same energy as one gallon of gasoline," can only make 17 miles.[9]

The United States is the only nation in the history of the world that has created wealth through the production of goods and services, rather than by pilfering from its citizens. All the monarchs, czars, emperors, and other leaders of the past have always amassed wealth for themselves and their nations by taking it from somebody else, including their own population. Now it seems that our government, led by Democrats, is mimicking the past, stealing everything we have earned and built.

We have also abandoned common sense and reason in favor of rule through feelings. This lack of logical rule has led to laws that attempt to control everything we do or say. Freedom of speech and of religion has come under heavy attack from the left, unless they want to practice freedom of speech for their own purposes.

We are marching steadily down a treacherous path, and Democrats are leading us to our destruction by our hands while Republicans remain tongue-tied and glassy-eyed. I cannot put enough emphasis on the word "treacherous." Democrats are pressing communist ideologies on us unmercifully, and if they ever totally succeed in getting absolute power, billions of deaths will ensue, and those who survive will be living in hell on earth. This is the hidden and most sinister agenda. It will give Democrats the pretext to seize total control over a world that is much reduced in population. Notice I didn't say they could do so efficiently. Our government doesn't do anything efficiently, and it never will.

Democrat wolves want all to believe that they are simply trying to create that illusive utopia, and we all are led to believe that utopias are wonderful paradises on earth. They are not even close, and the historic models of utopias illustrate that well. Utopias are inherently totalitarian, a state that controls "every aspect of organized life." The ruling party "attains this objective with the assistance of a security police . . . with unrestricted powers."[10] Plato's creation of utopia was designed to "avoid tyranny," but in the end, he created a "totalitarian City destructive of human nature."[11] Thomas More's *Utopia* "is a tyrannical society, destructive of individual sovereignty and free will."[12] The same holds true of Thomas Hobbe's utopian society in *Leviathan*; it is "totalitarian."[13]

Statism, or the control of everything by the state, is the obvious goal of Democrats, but that ideology closely resembles communism. Leon Trotsky, who was feared by Joseph Stalin and whom Stalin ordered murdered, opined that "in a country where the sole employer is the state, opposition means slow starvation."[14] In the words of Mark Levin, "America has been transitioning to a centralized, administrative statism that has become a power unto itself."[15]

Why does the Democratic Party press onward toward the impossible dream when even the older socialist states, most notably Russia and China, have been abandoning economic communism because they recognize it has failed them? One of the largest states in the world, China, began to give up the ghost of communism under Deng Ziaoping as long ago as 1979.[16] Just as China did, the Soviet Union, in the 1980s, recognized that communist ideologies were dysfunctional and began to alter course. Mikhail Gorbachev initiated *glasnost*, a relaxation of policies that had once suppressed free speech, and then Gorbachev "ended the monopoly of the Communist Party."[17]

According to Richard Pipes, communism failed for two main reasons, but one of them was that in order to "enforce equality," which is at the core of Marxist ideology, it became "necessary to create a coercive apparatus" that in the final analysis "negates equality."[18] Mark Levin poses excellent questions on the subject that begin with "when and how" will we know that "equality has been achieved?" What defines "equality," and how can it be measured? And who is the final arbiter on how it is measured?[19] True equality is but an "illusion,"[20] and those questions are rhetorical, impossible to answer.

It is a very unfortunate part of life that poor people have existed in every single society since the beginnings of recorded history. It has already been proven that Obama's policies increased the number of poor people in America by more than 8 million, rather than making them his equal. This trend will continue as the Democratic Party becomes more despotic. On the other hand, in democratic republics, such as the United States once was, the poor still have much more opportunity than they would have in a despotic state, a so-called utopia.[21] America's economic system "creates wealth and opportunity . . . more than any other system."[22]

If we continue on this path of allowing Democrats to oppress American citizens, the United States, like the Roman Empire, will eventually collapse under the weight of totalitarian and corrupt rule. In its stead, one will find the rich and the powerful lording over the peasantry, the masses who will have nothing. The communists in Hollywood and on CNN will be in for a huge surprise at that point. They will no longer have the power and wealth they have today, yet they blindly support efforts to destroy our country. When they are no longer needed, they will be banished to the hinterlands, and movie screens and televisions will grow dark.

The vast majority of the populace that professes support for statism will also be chagrined to discover that equality means they will have nothing. Remember the carrot and the mule? Once absolute power is established, the carrot will be removed; the ruse will no longer be necessary. The poor and the dispossessed have been misled by Democrats for more than a century, but it is only because they have told many convincing tales, much like Andrew Jackson told Indians and whites it was safest for both of them if Indians were removed to the Indian Territory.

Democrats were, and remain, the party of institutionalized racism. In the three decades leading up to the American Civil War, Democrats wholeheartedly supported the institution of slavery. For an entire century after the war, Democrats aggressively opposed any attempts at granting civil rights to all Americans. The only reason they appear to have switched their position on civil rights is to garner the minority vote. If not for that, they would care little for any minority. Since the days of Margaret Sanger's birth control crusade, they have subtly supported any move that entails selective breeding. Sanger, like Adolf Hitler, desired a master race free of mental or physical handicaps. Her efforts to curb population growth were intended for all but the white race. All members of the KKK were Democrats. Senator Robert Byrd of West Virginia, who is worshipped by the party elite, was a leader in the KKK. While statues of southern Civil War heroes are being removed from sight, Senator Byrd's name remains in evidence on numerous buildings and other places in the state of West Virginia. President Wilson was a racist. LBJ was, too. But it serves the Democratic Party's agenda better to attack Thomas Jefferson, a man who hoped to see the end of slavery. After all, if they can completely destroy Jefferson's overall legacy, they can dismantle the Constitution.

Crooked political "machines" that pilfered the coffers of America's largest cities were almost exclusively staffed by Democrats, and they wholeheartedly excluded African Americans from their "good ole boys clubs."[23] LBJ was an avowed racist who signed the Civil Rights Act of

1964 only to gain support from the African American voters in that year's election. It did not stop him from using the "n" word routinely.

According to Democrats, your assets belong to the state. In other words, to the Democratic Party. They actually believe that their so-called benevolence led to your success. You did not study hard and work hard to succeed; Democrats made you what you are.

Liberal college professors of the humanities enjoy telling their students that all democracies eventually collapse and are replaced by socialist governments. No historical precedence for that phenomenon exists. It's been the other way around. Russia, China, Vietnam, and other communist states have abandoned Marxist economic dogma in favor of capitalist principles. But those professors have to lie to the students to further the cause of the Democratic Party wolves. The only way that our nation can become a full-blown socialist state is if it is forced upon us, just as it was forced on Russians and Chinese. There will be no natural collapse of democracy.

Our politicians, most especially Democrats, are bent on trashing the Constitution and replacing it with a tool that gives them totalitarian powers. We have heard them describe themselves as progressives, a term that applied to the administrations of Teddy Roosevelt, William Howard Taft, and Woodrow Wilson. Wilson, so long ago, decried the fact that the "Constitution and the Bill of Rights was an impediment to progressive society."[24] What he really meant was that he could not usurp powers that our leaders were never intended to have, a sentiment also expressed by Barack Obama. Why do they want more power?

Democrats call it socialism, but in truth, it is statism, but both of the ideologies closely parallel communism, the most dysfunctional political and economic system ever foisted on the world. Once the system is fully in place, they will shed their sheep's clothing, revealing their true nature. This work is as much a warning to the poor and the lower middle class as it is to the middle and upper-middle class. Under communism, the poor will lose any and all opportunity to rise to another social level, nor will we all become equal. The entire middle class, detested by Democrats, will simply sink to the bottom. We will return to that feudal state of the Low Middle Ages (500 A.D. to 1000 A.D.), but it will be far more brutal than it was 1500 years ago.[25]

Laws that have been wholeheartedly supported by Democrats for more than one hundred years are clearly designed to destroy the greatest democracy in the history of the world. Their attacks, inspired by Karl Marx, include the destruction of the middle class, the suppression of religion, especially Christianity, and the ruination of the traditional family. Look around you and you can see the fruits of their labors in so many corners of our lives. The middle class is being systematically taxed out of existence. As evidenced by the actions of Georgetown University, we must hide in shame of our Christian beliefs. As if divorces have not done enough damage to families, we are being forced to believe that all sorts of aberrations that are the hallmarks of a decadent society are natural.

Severe damage has already been inflicted on our nation since the beginning of the last century, damage that will never be easy to remedy. Also, there is absolutely no way that we can instantaneously dismantle all of the left-wing institutions that already threaten our freedoms. But we can start by ferreting out the wolves from among the sheep, casting them out of the pasture. We can do this at the ballot box. All of us, whether white, African American, Hispanic, Asian American, Pacific Islander, and others, must awaken to reality. Democrats are sneaking about, deliberately frightening millions into supporting them for promises that they will never deliver. In the end, they will simply take everything from us and horde it for themselves. You, the voter, will get nothing.

End Notes

Introduction

1. CraigD.Idso,RobertM.Carter,andS.FredSinger. *Why Scientists Disagree About Global Warming* (ArlingtonHeights, Illinois:The HeartlandInstitute,2015)

2. Richard Pipes. *Communism: A History* (New York: Modern Library, 2003) 33, 55-56.

3. Matt Margolis and Mark Noonan, Matthew Souders, ed. T*he Worst President in History: The Legacy of Barack Obama.* (United States: Victory Books, 2016) 33-34.

4. Walter C. Kidney, Editor, Prepared under the direction of Laurence Urdang. *Webster's 21st Century Dictionary of the English Language* (Nashville: Thomas Nelson Publishers, 1993) 954.

5. Mark R. Levin. *Ameritopia: The Unmaking of America* (New York, London, Toronto, Sydney and New Delhi: Threshold Editions, 2012) 123.

6. Pipes. *Communism*, 158.

7. Karl Marx and Friedrich Engels, Joseph Katz, ed. *The Communist Manifesto* (New York, London, Toronto and Sydney: Pocket Books, 1964).

8. Ibid, 95

9. Pipes. *Communism*. 150.

10. Levin. *Ameritopia*. 6-7.

Chapter 1

1. Tim Hains. *RealClearPolitics* "Obama: Forget the Difference Between Capitalism and Communism, "Just Decide What Works"." 25 March 2016. https://www.realclearpolitics.com/video/2016/03/25/obama forget_the_difference_between_capitalism_and_communism_just_decide_what_works.html. Accessed 20 April 2018.

2. Walter C. Kidney, Editor, Prepared under the direction of Laurence Urdang. *Webster's 21st Century Dictionary of the English Language* (Nashville: Thomas Nelson Publishers, 1993) 250.

3. Ibid., 58.

4. Richard Pipes. *Communism: A History* (New York: Modern Library 2003) 16.

5. Ibid., 61.

6. Brian Kilmeade and Don Yeager. *Thomas Jefferson and the Tri- poli Pirates: The Forgotten War that Changed American History.* (New York: Sentinel, 2015) 14-15.

7. Mark R. Levin. *Ameritopia: The Unmaking of America* (New York, London, Toronto, Sydney and New Delhi: Threshold Editions) 189-198.

8. Ibid., 198-207.

9. Pipes. *Communism*. 42-48.

10. Allan H. Ryskind. *Hollywood Traitors: Blacklisted Screenwriters, Agents of Stalin, Allies of Hitler* (New York: Regnery Publish- ing, 2015) 169-185.

11. Pipes. *Communism*. 4.

12. Ibid., 6-7.

13. Levin. *Ameritopia*. 210.

14. Ibid., 22-23.

Chapter 2

1. Douglas Ernst. *WND*. "Bernie Scorched for Saying Whites 'Don't Know' Poverty." 7 March 2016. http://www.wnd.com/2016/03/fans-maul-sanders-for-say- ing-whites-dont-know-poverty/ Accessed 21 April 2018.

2. Jon Meacham. *American Lion: Andrew Jackson in the White House* (New York: Random House, 2008) 44-45.

3. Ibid.

4. Ibid.

5. John Ferling. *Jefferson and Hamilton: The Rivalry that Forged a Nation* (New York, London, New Delhi and Sydney: Bloomsbury Press, 2013) 33, 49, 53-56, 173. Ron Chernow. *Alexander Hamilton* (New York: The Penguin Press, 2004) 210-213, 312. Stephen E. Ambrose. *Undaunted Courage: Meriwether Lewis, Thomas Jefferson, and the Opening of the American West* (New York, London, Toronto and Sydney: Simon and Schuster Paperbacks, 1996) 34-35.

6. Ambrose. *Undaunted Courage*. 36-37.

7. Meacham. *American Lion*. 317-318.

8. Dinesh D'Souza. *Hillary's America: The Secret History of the Democratic Party* (Washington, D. C.: Regnery Publishing, 2016) 41-43.

9. Mark R. Levin. *Ameritopia: The Unmaking of America* (New York, London, Toronto, Sydney and New Delhi: Threshold Editions, 2012) 11. Richard Pipes. *Communism: A History* (New York: Modern Library, 2003) 95.

10. Levin. *Ameritopia*. 80-81.

11. Ibid., 211.

12. Ibid., 75

13. Pipes. *Communism*. 29.

Chapter 3

1. Karl Marx and Friedrich Engels, Joseph Katz, ed. *The Communist Manifesto* (New York, London, Toronto and Sydney: Pocket Books, 1964) 94.

2. Ibid., 85-86.

3. Charlie Spiering. "Obama's Historic Land Grab: 553 Million Acres for 'Conservation." 29 Dec 2016. http://www.breit- bart.com/big-government/2016/12/29/obamas-historic- land-grab-553-million-acres-conservation/ Accessed 5 November 2017.

4. Nancy Gibbs and Michael Duffy. *The President's Club: Inside the World's Most Exclusive Fraternity.* (New York, London, Toronto, Sydney, and New Delhi: Simon and Schuster Paper- backs, 2012) 43-44.

5. Mark R. Levin. *Ameritopia: The Unmaking of America* (New York, London, Toronto, Sydney and New Delhi: Threshold Editions, 2012) 187-188, 195-198.

6. Ibid., 131.

7. Ibid., 89.

8. Patrick J. Connolly. John Locke, *Internet Encyclopedia of Philosophy.* http://www.iep.utm.edu/locke/#SH4a. Accessed 13 February 2017.

Chapter 4

1. Karl Marx and Friedrich Engels, ed. Joseph Katz. The Com- munist Manifesto (New York, London, Toronto and Sydney: Pocket Books, 1964) 94.

2. Edward Gibbon. The Decline and Fall of the Roman Empire. (New York: Tess Press, 1963) 96, 162-163, 170, 281-285.

3. Marx and Engels. *The Communist Manifesto*, 9.

4. Mark R. Levin. Ameritopia: The Unmaking of America (New York, London, Toronto, Sydney and New Delhi: Threshold Editions, 2012) 14.

5. Ibid., 130-131.

6. Richard Brookhiser. James Madison (New York: Basic Books, 2011) 27-28.

7. Ibid., 213-214, 265-269.

8. Doris Kearns Goodwin. Team of Rivals: The Political Genius of Abraham Lincoln (New York, London, Toronto and Sydney: Simon and Schuster Paperbacks, 2005, 2006) 461-62.

9. Myles Dungan. How the Irish Won the West (New York: Sky-horse Publishing, 2011) 178-179.

10. Erin H. Hunter, ed. Outlaw Tales of the Old West: Fifty True Stories of Desperados, Crooks, Criminals, and Bandits. (Guilford, Connecticut and Helena, Montana: TwoDot, And Imprint of Rowman & Littlefield, 2016) 146-152.

11. FindLawForLegalProfessionals. Pollock v. Farmer's Loan and Trust Co. https://caselaw.findlaw.com/us-supreme- court/158/601.html Accessed 21 April 2018.

12. Reference.com. https://www.reference.com/government politics/underwood-tariff-act-b4a8405dc94d92d4 Accessed 21 April 2018.

13. Levin. Ameritopia. 214.

14. Dinesh D'Souza. Stealing America (New York: Broadside Books, 2015) 229.

15. John E. Clark. The Fall of the Duke of Duval (Austin, Texas: Eakin Press, 1999) 42-60.

16. Levin. Ameritopia. 234-239.

17. Ibid.

18. Ibid., 104.

Chapter 5

1. Karl Marx and Friedrich Engels, ed. Joseph Katz. *The Communist Manifesto* (New York, London, Toronto and Sydney: Pocket Books, 1964) 94.

2. Ibid., 85-86.

3. Quoted in Dinesh D'Souza. Stealing America (New York: Broadside Books, 2015) 147.

4. Claytee D. White. BlackPast.org: Remembered and Re claimed. "Walker, Madam C. J. (Sarah Breedlove), 1867- 1919." http://www.blackpast.org/aah/walker-madam-c-j-1867-1919 Accessed 13 October 2017.

5. Robert N. Gordon. "Why President Obama's estate tax proposal is a big deal." 6 February 2015 http://www.investment-news.com/article/20150206/REG/150209944/why-presiden t-obama Accessed 31 May 2017.

6. Peter Baker. The New York Times, "House Votes to Repeal Estate Tax" (New York: 16 April 2015) https://www.ny- times.com/2015/04/17/us/politics/house-votes-to-repeal-es- tate-tax.html?_r=0 Accessed 31 May 2017.

7. D'Souza. Stealing America, 165.

8. Marx and Engels, 81.

Chapter 6

1. Karl Marx and Friedrich Engels, ed. Joseph Katz. *The Communist Manifesto* (New York, London, Toronto and Sydney: Pocket Books, 1964) 94.

2. Mark R. Levin. Ameritopia: The Unmaking of America (New York, London, Toronto, Sydney and New Delhi: Threshold Editions, 2012) 216.

3. Gary Pecquet. "Private Property and Government Under the Constitution: Modern Intellectuals Do Not Take Private Property Seriously." https://fee.org/articles/private-property-and-government-under-the-constitution/ Accessed 15 October 2017.

4. Levin. Ameritopia. 216.

5. Ibid., 216-222.

6. C. Stone Brown, ed. Elihu Rosenblatt. Third World Traveler. "Legislating Repression: The Federal Crime Bill and the Anti-Terrorism and Effective Death Penalty Act," (South End Press, 1996) http://www.thirdworldtraveler.com/Prison_System/LegislatingRepression.html Accessed 7 June 2017.

7. Ibid.

8. Executive Order 11490, https://www.marxists.org history/usa/government president/1969/10/executive-order-11490/...Accessed 7 June 2017.

9. Matt Margolis and Mark Noonan, Matthew Souders, ed. The Worst President in History: The Legacy of Barack Obama. (United States: Victory Books, 2016) 33-34.

10. John E. Clark. The Fall of the Duke of Duval (Austin, Texas: Eakin Press, 1999) 290-315.

Chapter 7

1. Karl Marx and Friedrich Engels, ed. Joseph Katz. The Communist Manifesto (New York, London, Toronto and Sydney: Pocket Books, 1964) 94.

2. Mark R. Levin. Ameritopia: The Unmaking of America (New York, London, Toronto, Sydney and New Delhi: Threshold Editions, 2012) 153-154.

3. Ron Chernow. Alexander Hamilton, (New York: The Penguin Press, 2004) 344-361. John Ferling. Jefferson and Hamilton: The Rivalry that Forged a Nation (New York, London, New Delhi and Sydney: Bloomsbury Press, 2013) 214-221.

4. Richard Brookhiser. James Madison (New York: Basic Books, 2011) 225-226.

5. Jon Meacham. American Lion: Andrew Jackson in the White House (New York: Random House, 2008) 208. Ronald C. White, Jr. A. Lincoln: A Biography (New York: Random House Trade Paperbacks, 2010) 89.

6. George Brown Tindall and David Emory Shi. America: A Narrative History, Brief Ninth Edition (New York and Lon- don: W. W. Norton and Company, 2013) 745-746.

7. Matt Margolis and Mark Noonan, Matthew Souders, ed. The Worst President in History: The Legacy of Barack Obama. (United States: Victory Books, 2016) 42-43.

8. Hans Bader. "Clinton Pressure to Promote Affordable Housing Led to Mortgage Meltdown," https://cei.org/blog/clin-ton-pressure-promote-affordable-housing-led-mortgage-me ltdown Accessed 19 June 2017.

Chapter 8

1. Richard Pipes. Communism: A History (New York: Modern Library, 2003) 69-72.

2. Mark R. Levin. Ameritopia: The Unmaking of America (New York, London, Toronto, Sydney and New Delhi: Threshold Editions, 2012) 36, 48, and 64.

3. Karl Marx and Friedrich Engels, ed. Joseph Katz. The Communist Manifesto (New York, London, Toronto and Sydney: Pocket Books, 1964) 94.

4. David Wallechinsky. "AllGov: Everything Our Government Really Does," Federal Communications Commission. http://www.allgov.com/departments/independent-agencies/federal-communications-commission Accessed 4 July 2017.

5. Wikipedia. "Amateur radio operator." https://en.wikipedia.org/wiki/Amateur_radio_operator Accessed 4 July 2017.

6. Allan H. Ryskind. Hollywood Traitors: Blacklisted Screenwriters, Agents of Stalin, Allies of Hitler (New York: Regnery Publishing, 2015) xix, 5, 27 and 389-90.

7. Ann Coulter. Treason: Liberal Treachery from the Cold War to the War on Terrorism (New York: Crown Forum, 2003) 34.

8. "Ham Radio Regulations." http://w5yi.org/page.php?id=57 Accessed 4 July 2017.

Chapter 9

1. Karl Marx and Friedrich Engels, ed. Joseph Katz. The Com- munist Manifesto (New York, London, Toronto and Sydney: Pocket Books, 1964) 94.

2. Allan H. Ryskind. Hollywood Traitors: Blacklisted Screenwriters, Agents of Stalin, Allies of Hitler (New York: Regnery Publishing, 2015) 133. Sinan Toprak, "What did Stalin's Collectivisation of Agriculture in the USSR do in the Long Term?" https://www.quora.com/What-did-Stalins-collectivisation- of-agriculture-in-the-USSR-do-in-the-long-term Accessed 7 July 2017.

3. Richard Pipes. Communism: A History (New York: Modern Library, 2003) 61.

4. Terence Kealey. The Telegraph. "DDT is safe: just ask the professor who ate it for 40 years." http://www.telegraph.co.uk/comment/4264030/DDT-is-safe-just-ask-the-professor- who-ate -it-for-40-years.html Accessed 16 October 2017.

5. Robert Zubrin. The New Atlantis, "The Truth About DDT and Silent Spring" http://www.thenewatlantis.com/publica- tions/the-truth-about-ddt-and-silent-spring Accessed 7 July 2017.

6. Mandy Mayfield. Washington Examiner. "Bill Nye: Older people need to 'die' out before climate science can advance." 19 July 2017. https://washingtonexaminer.com/bill-nye-older-people-need-to-die-out-before-climate-science-can- advance Accessed 23 April 2018.

7. Pipes. Communism. 60-62.

8. Ibid., 58-59.

9. Stanley Fischer, author, Olivier Jean Blanchard, Kenneth A. Froot, and Jeffrey D. Sachs, editors. National Bureau of Eco- nomic Research, The Transition in Eastern Europe, Volume 1, "Russia and the Soviet Union, Then and Now" http://www.nber.org/chapters/c6021 pages 221-258. Accessed 9 July 2017.

10. Patrick Hedger. Freedom Works. The Chevrolet Volt: The Only 30 Percent-Off Car in America That is Still a Bad Deal. http://www.freedomworks.org/content/chevrolet-volt-only- 30-percent-car-america-still-bad-deal Accessed 11 July 2017.

11. Margaret Thatcher. http://www.snopes.com/politics/quotes/thatcher.asp Accessed 26 August 2017.

12. Pipes. Communism. 16.

Chapter 10

1.Karl Marx and Friedrich Engels, ed. Joseph Katz. The Communist Manifesto (New York, London, Toronto and Sydney: Pocket Books, 1964) 94.

2. Richard Pipes. Communism: A History (New York: Modern Library, 2003) 59.

3. Ibid., 38-39.

4. Associated Press. Washington Post. "20 CIO Aides Cited as Having Police Records," December 3, 1941, 1, cited in Craig Shirley. December 1941: 31 Days that Changed America and Saved the World (Nashville: Nelson Books, 2013) 48.

5. Pipes. Communism. 84-87.

6. David Brinkley. Washington Goes to War (New York: Alfred A. Knopf, 1988) 17, cited in Craig Shirley. December 1941: 31 Days that Changed America and Saved the World (Nashville: Nelson Books, 2013) 48.

7. The Free Dictionary by Farlex. Affirmative Action. http://legal-dictionary.thefreedictionary.com/ Affirmative+Action Accessed 19July 2017.

8. http://www.casebriefs.com/blog/law/constitutional-law/constitutional-law-keyed-to-chemerinsky/equal-protection/regents-of-the-university-of-california-v-bakke/ Accessed 19 July 2017.

9. Ballotpedia, "California Affirmative Action, Proposition 209, https://ballotpedia.org/CaliforniaAffirmative Action, Proposition 209 (1996) Accessed 19 July 2017.

10. Mark R. Levin. Ameritopia: The Unmaking of America (New York, London, Toronto, Sydney and New Delhi: Threshold Editions, 2012) 5.

Chapter 11

1. Karl Marx and Friedrich Engels, ed. Joseph Katz. The Communist Manifesto (New York, London, Toronto and Sydney: Pocket Books, 1964) 94.

2. Thought Co. "World Population Growth," https://www.thoughtco.com/current-world-population- 1435270 Accessed 19 July 2017.

3. Gerhard Peters and John T. Woolley. Richard Nixon: "Executive Order 11647-Federal Regional Councils," February 10, 1972. The American Presidency Project. http://www.presidency.ucsb.edu/ws/?pid=106739 Accessed 19 July 2017. Peters and Woolley. Richard Nixon: "Executive Order 11731-Amending Executive Order No. 11647 Relating to Federal Regional Councils," July 23, 1973. The American Presidency Project. http://www.presidency.ucsb.edu/ws/?pid=106767 Accessed 19 July 2017.

4. David Bay. The United States of America Officially Abolished the Individual States in 1972!. Cutting Edge Ministries. http://www.cuttingedge.org/news/n1179.cfm Accessed 19 July 2017.

5.United States Code. "Reorganization Plan No. 7 of 1949," https://www.govregs.com/uscode/appendix5a_reorganiza- tionplans4_reorganizationplan18 Accessed 19 July 2017.

6. Richard Pipes. Communism: A History (New York: Modern Library, 2003) 49.

7. Marx and Engels. The Communist Manifesto, 90-91.

8. Pipes. Communism. 130-131.

9. Tom Clancy. A Clear and Present Danger (New York: Berkley Books, 1989) Title.

Chapter 12

1. Karl Marx and Friedrich Engels, ed. Joseph Katz. The Communist Manifesto (New York, London, Toronto and Sydney: Pocket Books, 1964), 94.

2. Laura Meckler and Josh Mitchell. The Wall Street Journal. "Hillary Clinton Proposes Debt-Free Tuition at Public Col- leges." 10 August 2015 https://www.wsj.com /articles/ hillary-clinton-proposes-debt-free-tuition-at-public-colleges-14391 79200 Accessed 24 April 2018.

3. Ronald C. White, Jr. A. Lincoln: A Biography (New York: Random House, 2010) 199, 280-281.

4. Liberty Zone Café. "Are Americans Practicing Communism?" http://www.libertyzone.com/Communist-Mani- festo-Planks.html Accessed 23 December 2016.

5. Richard Pipes. Communism: A History (New York: Modern Library, 2003) 130-131.

Chapter 13

1. Michael Crichton. State of Fear (New York: Avon Books, 2004) Title.

2. Richard Pipes. Communism: A History (New York: Modern Democratic Party Elitest Library, 2003) 63-68.

3. Sean Wilentz. New York Times. "Lincoln And Douglass Had It Right," 16 September 2015. Frederick Douglass, David W. Blight, ed. Narrative of the Life of Frederick Douglass: An American Slave (Boston and New York: Bedford/St. Martin's, 2003) 168-170. Ronald C. White, Jr. A. Lincoln: A Biography (New York: Random House, 2010) 76, 312, 653-654.

4. Mark R. Levin. Ameritopia: The Unmaking of America (New York, London, Toronto, Sydney and New Delhi: Threshold Editions, 2012) 233.

5. Ibid., 24, 28-29.

6. Matt Margolis. The Scandalous Presidency of Barack Obama (New York and Nashville: Post Hill Press, 2018) 28.

7. Kelsey Snell. The Washington Post. "18 million would lose insurance in the first year of Obamacare repeal without re- placement, CBO report says," 17 January 2017. https://www.washingtonpost.com/news/powerpost/wp/2017/01/17/18-million-would-lose-insurance-in-first-year-of-obamacare-repeal-without-replacement-cbo-report-says/?utm_term=.05e05fffc7db Accessed 29 November 2017.

8.Dan Mangan. CNBC. "Obamacare repeal would lead to 24 million more people without health insurance" 13 June 2016. https://cnbc.com/2016/06/13/obamacare-repeal-would- lead-to-24-million-more-people-without-health- insurance.html Accessed 29 November 2017. Louis Jacobson. POLITIFACT. "What would the impact be if the Affordable Care Act is repealed?" 5 January 2017. http://www.politifact.com/truth-o-meter/article/2017/jan/05/what-would-be-impact-if-affordable-care-act-repeal/ Accessed 29 November 2017.

9. Tami Luhby. CNN. "32 million people would lose coverage if Obamacare was repealed," 30 June 2017. http://money.cnn.com/2017/06/30/news/economy/obamacare-repeal-trump/index.html Accessed 29 November 2017.

10. Gary Pecquet. "Private Property and Government Under the Constitution: Modern Intellectuals Do Not Take Private Property Seriously." https://fee.org/articles/private-property-and-government-under-the-constitution/ Accessed 15 October 2017.

11. Karl Marx and Friedrich Engels, ed. Joseph Katz. The Communist Manifesto (New York, London, Toronto and Sydney: Pocket Books, 1964) 91-92.

12. Jim Iovino. "Jesus Missing from Obama's Georgetown Speech: White House asked university to cover symbol." http://www.nbcwashington.com/news/archive/Jesus-Missing-From-Obamas-Georgetown-Speech.html Accessed 24 July 2017.

13. EastWest.edu. Sub-Saharan Monitor, Somalia Iran Terrorism. "Somalia Government warns US over al-Shabaab uranium traffic with Iran" 5 September 2017. https://eastwest.eu/en/ opinioni/sub-saharan-monitor/somalia-govt-warns-us-over- al-shabaab-uranium-traffic-with-iran Accessed 24 April 2018.

14. Brian Kilmeade and Don Yaeger. Thomas Jefferson and the Tripoli Pirates: The Forgotten War That Changed American History (New York: Sentinel, 2015) 14-15.

15. Marx and Engels. 93.

16. Ibid. 95.

17. Allan H. Ryskind. Hollywood Traitors: Blacklisted Screenwriters, Agents of Stalin, Allies of Hitler (New York, Regnery Publishing, 2015) 423.

18. Levin. Ameritopia. 27.

19. Dinesh D'Souza. Hillary's America: The Secret History of the Democratic Party (Washington, D. C.: Regnery Publishing, 2016) 164-165.

20. Levin. Ameritopia. 137.

21. Energy and Opportunity. "Hydraulic Fracturing: Unlocking America's Natural Gas Resources," http://www.hydraulic- fracturing.com/#/?section=energy-and-opportunity Accessed 24 July 2017.

22. Ron Chernow. Alexander Hamilton, (New York: The Penguin Press, 2004) 7.

23. The Center for Legislative Archives. "San Francisco Earth quake, 1906," https://www.archives.gov/legislative/features/sf. Accessed 24 July 2017.

24. Statistic Brain. "Earthquake Statistics," http://www.statistic- brain.com/earthquake-statics/. Accessed 24 July 2017.

25. Daniel Yergin. The Prize: The Epic Quest for Oil, Money, & Power (New York: Touchstone, 1991, 1992) 82.

26. Diana Davids Olien and Roger M. Olien. Oil in Texas: The Gusher Age, 1895-1945 (Austin: University of Texas Press, 2002) 1.

27. Dee Brown. The American West. (New York, London, Toronto, Sydney, Tokyo, and Singapore: Charles Scribner's Sons, 1994) 158.

Chapter 14

1. nasa.gov graph in Michael Crichton. State of Fear (New York: Avon Books, 2004) 95.

2. Heat Sheet. "Obama's 'Cow Farts' Climate Speech: All Left-Wing Dogma, Sparse Science." https://heatst.com/politics/ obamas-cow-farts-climate-speech-all-left-wing-dogma- sparse-science/ Accessed 22 July 2017.

3. Quote from Ashley Judd's tirade on CNN.

4. Nathaniel Philbrick. Valiant Ambition: George Washington, Benedict Arnold, and the Fate of the American Revolution (New York: Viking, 2016) 136.

5. Philbrick. Valiant Ambition. 211-213. Ron Chernow. Alexander Hamilton, (New York: The Penguin Press, 2004) 114.

6. Ronald C. White, Jr. A. Lincoln: A Biography (New York: Random House, 2009) 157.

7. Ibid., 182

8. Philbrick. Valiant Ambition. 218-219.

9. White. A. Lincoln. 62.

10. Dee Brown. The American West. (New York, London, Toronto, Sydney, Tokyo, and Singapore: Charles Scribner's Sons, 1994) 146.

11. Ibid., 146-147.

12. Craig D. Idso, Robert M. Carter, and S. Fred Singer. Why Scientists Disagree About Global Warming (Arlington Heights, Illinois: The Heartland Institute, 2015) 7-31.

13. Ibid. 31.

14. Ibid. 42.

15. Ibid. 91, 95-96.

16. Ibid. 76-77.

17. Matt Margolis. The Scandalous Presidency of Barack Obama (New York and Nashville: Post Hill Press, 2018) 59-64, 119- 123.

18. Deroy Murdock. Newsmax. "Obama's 'green projects bleed red ink." 20 July 2012. http://www.newsmax.com/Mur-dock/obama-green-jobs/2012/07/20/id/446027/ Accessed 20 October 2017.

19. Margolis. The Scandalous Presidency of Barack Obama. 45-48.

20. 20. New England Historical Society. "The Deadly, Mostly For- gotten Heat Wave of 1896." http://www.newenglandhistori- calsociety.com/deadly-mostly-forgotten-heat-wave-1896/ Accessed 28 July 2017.

21. Los Angeles Times. "Down the Decades with Los Angeles." December 4, 1941, 22, cited in Craig Shirley. December 1941: 31 Days that Changed America and Saved the World (Nashville: Nelson Books, 2013) 84-85.

22. Gary Pecquet. "Private Property and Government Under the Constitution: Modern Intellectuals Do Not Take Private Property Seriously." https://fee.org/articles/private-property-and-government-under-the-constitution/ Accessed 15 October 2017.

Chapter 15

1. Ernest Hemingway. For Whom the Bell Tolls (New York, Lon- don, Toronto, Sydney, Tokyo, and Singapore: Scribner Paperback Fiction, Simon and Schuster, 1940) 339.

2. Richard Pipes. Communism: A History (New York: Modern Library, 2003) 147-148.

3. Dinesh D'Souza, Stealing America (New York: Broadside Books, 2015) 229.

4. Ibid. 239.

5. Mark R. Levin. Ameritopia: The Unmaking of America (New York, London, Toronto, Sydney and New Delhi: Threshold Editions, 2012) 215-223.

6. Hans Baumann. Newsmax. "The Truth About Green Energy," 11 November 2016. http://www.newsmax.com/Hans-Baumann/green-energy-wind-power-solar-power/2016/11/11/id/758402/ Accessed 24 October 2017.

7. Matt Ridley. The Spectator. "Wind turbines are neither clean nor green and they provide zero global energy." https://www.spectator.co.uk/s017/05/wind-turbines-are-neither-clean-nor-green-and-they-provide-zero-global-energy/ Accessed 24 October 2017.

8. Baumann. "The Truth About Green Energy."

9. Ibid.

10. Pipes. Communism. 105.

11. Levin. Ameritopia. 36.

12. Ibid., 49.

13. Ibid., 66.

14. Pipes. Communism. 152.

15. Levin. Ameritopia. 188.

16. Pipes. Communism. 131.

17. Ibid., 84-87.

18. Ibid., 154.

19. Levin. Ameritopia. 78.

20. Ibid., 104

21. Ibid., 132.

22. Ibid., 171.

23. Craig Shirley. December 1941: 31 Days that Changed America and Saved the World (Nashville: Nelson Books, 2013) 462.

24. Ibid. 466.

25. Karl Marx and Friedrich Engels, ed. Joseph Katz. The Communist Manifesto (New York, London, Toronto and Sydney: Pocket Books, 1964) 61-62.